CHEF'S SECRETS

Library of Congress Cataloging in Publication Number:
2004104631

ISBN: 1-59474-005-4

Printed in Singapore

Typeset in Chalet Comprime and Triplex

Designed by Bryn Ashburn

Distributed in North America by Chronicle Books
85 Second Street
San Francisco, CA 94105

10 9 8 7 6 5 4 3 2 1

Quirk Books
215 Church Street
Philadelphia, PA 19106
www.quirkbooks.com

The recipe on page 38 is reprinted with permission of
the author from Aquavit by Marcus Samuelsson, ©
2003 by Townhouse Restaurant Group, first published
by Houghton Mifflin Company, New York.

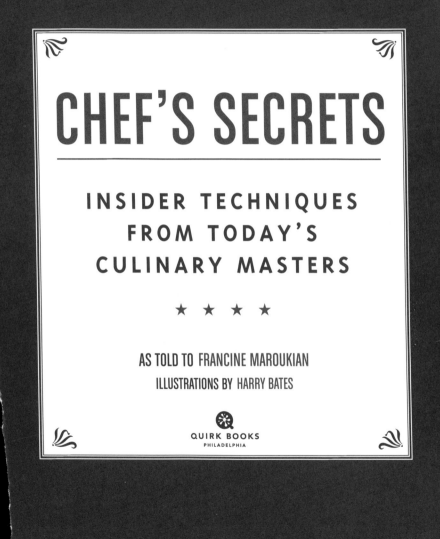

CHEF'S SECRETS

INSIDER TECHNIQUES FROM TODAY'S CULINARY MASTERS

★ ★ ★ ★

AS TOLD TO FRANCINE MAROUKIAN

ILLUSTRATIONS BY HARRY BATES

QUIRK BOOKS

PHILADELPHIA

TABLE OF CONTENTS

★ ★ ★ ★

INTRODUCTION

★ ★

When I started my New York City career as the catering director of the famous Silver Palate food store, the single most important piece of kitchen equipment in my life was the telephone. Despite what clients thought, I wasn't the catering chef—I only planned the menus and showed up at the parties to make sure that all went well. When I left the Silver Palate to open my own business, I thought I would do the same thing: take the calls, sell the parties, and use the deposit money to pay other people to do the cooking. However, when the first request that came in was for a fruit and cheese party in the prestigious Enoteca of the Italian Trade Commission, I didn't bother hiring anyone else. Three years at America's most important specialty foods store guaranteed that I could arrange platters with the best of them. The day the check from that job cleared the bank, I spread the money out on my desk and thought: I can do this—and if I can't, I should learn.

I toyed around with the idea of enrolling in cooking classes, but since my business appeared to be up and running, I settled for on-the-job training. Although my clients schooled me in the extravagances of Upper East Side etiquette, my practical culinary education came from the aspiring actors, singers, and other "theatre gypsies" who work as New York's freelance catering staff. During party season, if I was doing two jobs a week, they were doing ten. In an attempt to stockpile money for the slow months, catering waiters and kitchen people work doubles (lunch and a cocktail party or dinner) and sometimes even triples (throw in a corporate breakfast). Experienced in preparing and serving every kind of food for every sort of occasion, my staff arrived to work carrying not only the most fabulous gossip, but cooking tips they learned in many other kitchens. The first time one of them put a wet side towel under my cutting board, it was like a blow to my brain: "Oh, *that's* how you keep the damn thing from sliding all over a distressed Italian blue pearl granite counter!"

Passing cooking tips and shortcuts along (traditionally called "trucs," which is French for *trick*) is part of the legacy of professional kitchens. Although the practice may be an old one, the standard for what constitutes a "tip" has changed over the last ten years. As legions of people grew more passionate about cooking, chef's tips became a regular feature on a network of food television shows, as well as in magazines and cookbooks. Telling someone to roll a lemon around on the counter to extract more juice doesn't really cut it any longer, and so the chefs in this book were asked to go a step beyond common cooking knowledge. Some of their secrets are easy, some are hard; some you'll use, some you won't. And by no means is this one of those portentous encyclopedic volumes of every little thing. But, just as my catering staff did for me, these chefs will give you a behind-the-scenes peek into many different kitchens. You're on your own for the gossip.

AUTHOR'S SECRET:
HOW TO CLEAN AND CHOP PARSLEY

★ ★ ★ ★ ★ ★ ★ ★ ★ ★ ★ ★ ★ ★ ★ ★ ★ ★

In catering, there are some things you do as a matter of habit while setting up for every job: (1) make sure you have enough paper towels and trash bags, (2) cut lemons and limes for the bar, and (3) fine chop a pile of flat-leaf, or Italian, parsley. There is no telling how much parsley I have chopped in my career: We used it to add flavor, color, and a little freshness to almost every savory dish. In a way, you could say that chopped parsley is the little black dress of catering—it can cover a multitude of sins and goes with almost everything. I used to painstakingly wash and dry the parsley before chopping (which took forever because the leaves have to be bone-dry) until one of my waiters showed me this secret. Suddenly what used to take thirty minutes and a lot of counter space was reduced to five minutes and an area the size of a cutting board.

STEP ONE: Using one hand, gather the leafy ends of the parsley into a ball, rest it on a cutting board, and chop off the stems.

STEP TWO: Loosely holding the leafy ends together, bring the knife down across the ball several times to coarsely chop it. When the parsley is laying almost flat on the board (it will easier to manage when it loses its "spring"), the fine chopping can begin.

STEP THREE: Fine chop the parsley. Holding the tip of the knife with one hand (for balance, not pressure), start to chop, moving the blade of the knife in a rapid up-and-down motion (staccato) while moving the handle of your knife from side-to-side in an arc shape. Every ten or twelve chops, use the side of the blade to scrape the parsley back into a mound. Continue until the parsley is finely chopped.

STEP FOUR: Wash the parsley. Using the side of the blade like a spatula, transfer the chopped parsley to the center of a clean kitchen towel. Gather the ends together, slide your hand down to create a tube, and twist the towel until it forms a sealed ball around the parsley. Place the parsley ball under cool running water and let the water wash through the parsley ball until it runs pale (instead of bright) green. Wring the parsley ball (right through the towel), twisting out any extra water.

STEP FIVE: Place the towel in the middle of the cutting board and unwrap the ball. You will have a mound of finely chopped, perfectly clean, dry and fluffy parsley. Transfer to a small bowl and use to start your own catering business.

CHAPTER ONE

★ ★ ★ ★

TECHNIQUE

PROFILE

Steven Raichlen, who trained at Le Cordon Bleu and La Varenne in Paris, is one of the world's foremost authorities on live-fire cooking. Referred to by Oprah Winfrey as the "gladiator of grilling," he is the author of twenty-four books, including *The Barbecue Bible*, an encyclopedic study of worldwide techniques (and the result of his 150,000-mile odyssey to twenty-five countries on five continents), and *BBQ USA*, which might be described as *On the Road* meets regional American barbecue. He is the host and founder of Barbecue University, a cooking school and public television series devoted to grilling and barbecue, filmed on location at the Greenbrier resort in West Virginia.

HOW TO BUILD A THREE-ZONE FIRE ON A CHARCOAL GRILL

★ ★ ★ ★ ★ ★ ★ ★ ★ ★ ★ ★

When you are using a gas grill, you can adjust the heat by turning the knob. Easy enough. But on a charcoal fire, you need to establish three different heat "zones": searing, cooking, and safety.

STEP ONE: Light your charcoal. The "politically correct" way is to use a chimney starter (an upright divided metal cylinder). Place the charcoal in the top and a crumpled sheet of newspaper (or a paraffin fire starter) in the bottom and light. A wire partition will keep the charcoal from falling

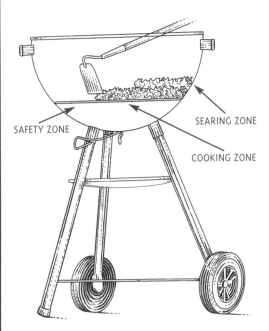

SAFETY ZONE

SEARING ZONE

COOKING ZONE

into the newspaper. The cylindrical shape of the chimney assures that all the coals will light evenly. The "bubba" way is to forego the chimney and douse the coals with lighter fluid or use self-lighting charcoal. In this case, make sure the coals are *completely* lit so you don't get a petroleum residue.

STEP TWO: Imagine your grill is divided into three equal parts.

STEP THREE: Divide the coals. Using a long-handled spatula or tongs, rake half the coals into a double layer at one side of the grill; this is your hot or searing zone. Rake the remaining coals into a single layer in the center; this is your cooking zone. Leave the remaining third of the grill free of coals; this is your cool or safety zone for warming food or dodging flare-ups.

MORE CHEF'S SECRETS . . .

FM: What's the difference between grilling and barbecue?
SR: Grilling is a fast, high-heat method done directly over the fire. True barbecue is an indirect method, done at a much lower temperature for a much longer time, with a heavy presence of wood smoke. Think hot sex versus long, slow lovemaking.

Foods you *grill* include steak, chicken breasts, fish filets, and vegetables; foods you *barbecue* tend to be larger or tougher cuts of meat, like brisket, ribs, turkeys, and pork shoulders.

FM: How do you get that cool crosshatch of grill marks?
SR: Place your steak, chops, or chicken breasts on the hot, clean, oiled grate. Grill for 1 to 3 minutes; then give the meat a quarter turn and continue cooking. *Voilà!* A crosshatch of grill marks.

FM: What are some of the stranger things you've grilled?
SR: Ice cream, by indirect grilling in a hollowed pineapple shell, topped with meringue. It's a grill jockey's version of baked Alaska that I call "baked Hawaii."

GRILLING TIPS FROM STEVE RAICHLEN

★ **Raichlen's Rules for Great Grilling: 1) Keep it hot.** Start with a hot grill grate. **2) Keep it clean.** Scrub your grate often with a stiff wire brush to prevent sticking. **3) Keep it lubricated.** Oil the grate with a paper towel folded into a pad and dipped in oil to prevent sticking and to produce killer grill marks.

★ To test the heat of a charcoal fire, use the Mississippi test. Hold your hand about 3 inches above the grate and start counting "one Mississippi, two Mississippi," and so on. You'll get to about "two Mississippi" before the heat forces you to move your hand over a hot fire; to about "five Mississippi" over a medium fire; and to "eight Mississippi" or "ten Mississippi" over a cool fire.

★ Use the Charmin test to determine when barbecued cabbage, onions, potatoes, squash, and other round vegetables are cooked: Squeeze the sides between your thumb and forefinger. When they are "squeezably" soft, the veggies are cooked.

★ Select lump charcoal (in fancy food stores and natural food super-markets) rather than briquettes. The latter contain coal dust, furniture scraps, borax, and petroleum binders.

★ Place flavorful liquids (such as vinegar or apple cider) in a spray bottle and use for basting your meat, ribs, and chicken.

★ When using a sweet barbecue sauce, apply it during the last 5 minutes—better yet, serve it on the side. This way, you won't burn the sugar in the sauce.

HOW TO MAKE DREDGING NEAT AND EASY

★ ★ ★ ★ ★ ★ ★ ★ ★ ★ ★ ★

When I was *chef tournant* at La Tulipe in New York's Greenwich Village, we cooked a lot of soft-shell crab. We soaked them in milk and then coated them by dipping them in flour (called dredging). Here is the method we used to keep our hands clean, which is also the best method to use for getting an even coating (for flour or breadcrumbs) on anything: fish filets, shrimp, scaloppine of veal or chicken, or even vegetables.

STEP ONE: Put a piece of parchment paper in a pie plate and then mound flour on top of the parchment.

STEP TWO: Place the item you are dredging in the center of the flour.

Sara MOULTON

★ ★ ★ ★ ★ ★ ★ ★

PROFILE

Sara Moulton is one of the hardest-working women in the food business, juggling three jobs as host of *Sara's Secrets* on the Food Network, chef of the executive dining room at *Gourmet* magazine, and food editor for ABC-TV's *Good Morning America*. After graduating from culinary school, Moulton worked in Boston and New York before taking a postgraduate stage with a master chef in Chartres, France, in 1979. Moulton, who also worked as sous chef at La Tulipe in New York, cofounded the New York Women's Culinary Alliance, an "old girl's network" that celebrated its twentieth anniversary in 2002. The author of *Sara Moulton Cooks at Home*, she lives in New York City with her husband and two children.

STEP THREE: Pick up each side of the parchment paper and lightly toss the item back and forth in the flour until it is coated. You will be amazed how much neater it is to coat both sides of the item by using the parchment rather than picking it up with your hands to turn it over.

When you are flouring smaller items (like scallops or vegetable sticks), transfer them to a wire mesh colander after coating and shake gently to remove excess flour.

MORE CHEF'S SECRETS . . .

FM: Name a piece of kitchen equipment you can't live without.
SM: Ten-inch Wusthof chef's knife.

FM: If you could have been a private chef to anyone in history, who would it be?
SM: Thomas Jefferson. He was totally cool, and I probably would have learned a lot from him.

FM: Do you have a piece of simple kitchen wisdom to share?
SM: Never apologize; never explain. When you have guests over for dinner, don't tell them what you did wrong—they are there to have a good time. Pretend it is the best meal you ever made.

HOW TO SLICE OR DICE WITH A VEGETABLE PEELER

★ ★ ★ ★ ★ ★ ★ ★ ★ ★ ★ ★

Andrew FRIEDMAN

Finding new applications for tools and equipment can be the gateway to discovering little tricks that make prep work efficient and enjoyable. For example, slicing or cutting vegetables down to minute size or thickness—for, say, carpaccio, salads, and soups—can feel like microsurgery when working with a knife. Solution: A vegetable peeler can do double duty as a stand-in for a mandoline to cut paper-thin slices of vegetables, or as a knife for cutting very small dice, making it easy to keep things nicely uniform without exercising Andre Agassi—like focus on each and every slice.

STEP ONE: First off, if you don't have a European-style vegetable peeler, get yourself one. These inexpensive peelers (most are produced in Switzerland) have a wider blade than swivel models. They give you greater control, especially for the uses described in the next steps.

STEP TWO: Peel the vegetable as you normally would. If the vegetable is round or oblong, use a knife to cut one side down to a level surface to ensure that all slices have the same shape and thickness, then slice a small piece off the opposite side so you can rest the vegetable flat without it wobbling. This will give you more uniform slices and also help keep the knife from slipping.

STEP THREE: Slice or dice the vegetable. To make thin slices: Simply pull the peeler along the

PROFILE

Andrew Friedman, a graduate of Columbia University and the French Culinary Institute's "La Technique" cooking program, is one of the premier collaborators in New York's cookbook-writing community, specializing in helping chefs and restaurateurs find their "voice" on the written page. Friedman coauthored *Alfred Portale's Gotham Bar and Grill Cookbook*, which won the IACP Cookbook Award for Best Chef or Restaurant Cookbook. In addition to his collaboration with Portale on two other books, he has worked with Pino Luongo, Tom Valenti, Laurent Tourondel, Bill Telepan, and Michael Lomonaco. He also wrote a cookbook based on the weekly *CBS Saturday Morning* segment "Chef on a Shoestring."

exposed edge of the vegetable. If the vegetable is wider than the blade, cut 2 or more slices, being sure not to overlap the cuts.

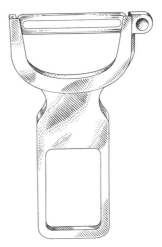

To make small dice: Use a sharp, thin-bladed paring knife to cut evenly spaced slits 2 inches into the vegetable. Then, cut 2-inch-deep slits perpendicular to these, forming a grid. Use the peeler to slice across the exposed surface of the vegetable down to where the slits end. The vegetable will fall in a tiny dice. Repeat this procedure until you get down to the root or use up all of the vegetable.

MORE CHEF'S SECRETS . . .

FM: Most underrated American restaurant city?
AF: Seattle.

FM: Who's a cooking legend?
AF: Wolfgang Puck. The first brilliant rule-breaker of his generation; a lot of our most famous chefs got their inspiration and courage from him.

FM: Silliest eighties food trend?
AF: Wasabi mashed potatoes.

HOW TO DETACH A STUCK CHEESE WRAPPER

★ ★ ★ ★ ★ ★ ★ ★ ★ ★ ★ ★

Max McCALMAN

★ ★ ★ ★ ★ ★ ★ ★

Paper wrappers can stick to the surface of any cheese, from soft to hard, making it a problem to present a whole wheel on a cheese tray or to cut and serve a wedge that isn't still adorned with paper. When cutting down into the body of the cheese, hopefully the wrapper will remain stuck to only one of the cut portions and you will be able to lift the other piece free of the wrapper. If it remains stuck, prying the wrapper off the cheese with the tip of a sharp knife may be the only solution. Learn it and spread the curd!

STEP ONE: Gently try to pull the paper off. Set the cheese down with the stuck wrapper facing down on the cutting board (or whatever you are using for preparing your tray, trolley, board, or other display) and try to remove the paper with your fingers. If this doesn't work, turn the cheese over and pry off a small portion of the wrapper— enough to cut through the rind directly without pushing the paper down into the cheese.

STEP TWO: Expose the wrapper. Cut out a wedge of cheese, going through top and bottom rind (so it pulls away) but stopping short of the paper. Lift up the cut portion, leaving the loosened wrapper on the cutting surface. At this point, the wrapper is exposed and ready to be peeled off.

STEP THREE: Scrape off the wrapper with a knife. If all else fails, use the edge of a sharp knife

PROFILE

Max McCalman's professional life revolves around sharing the pleasures of cheese with patrons of New York's Picholine and Artisanal. As *maître fromager*, he has become a staunch advocate for small, artisanal cheese producers around the world. With no formal training, McCalman owes his cheese expertise to the input and feedback of countless caesophiles he has met during the last nine years at Picholine, where he created the restaurant's now-famous cheese program with chef-proprietor Terrance Brennan. At Artisanal, Brennan's cheese-centric restaurant venture, McCalman was also instrumental in creating the initial cheese selections. He is the author of *The Cheese Plate*, his first book on the subject.

to carefully scrape away the wrapper, pressing down lightly so you do not damage the rind underneath.

MORE CHEF'S SECRETS . . .

FM: How do you get someone to be a little more adventurous when it comes to trying cheese?

MM: I mention that this is a great time of the year to enjoy this particular cheese or that the cheese is at a peak stage of ripeness. I may also point out that a cheese is somehow "endangered"—a "get-it-while-you-can" type.

FM: What is your favorite grilled cheese sandwich?

MM: I haven't had one in years, but I'd probably use Appleby's Cheshire and maybe nothing else besides some good bread.

FM: Fondue: fan or foe?

MM: Sounds like a fine idea in a chalet after an arduous day on the slopes, but I like cheeses by themselves, without melting them or stirring in other ingredients.

CHEESE TIPS FROM MAX McCALMAN

★ For appetizer plates of three to five cheeses, serve 1 to 1¹/2 ounces per person; for after-dinner plates of three to five cheeses, serve 1¹/4 to 1³/4 ounces per person.

★ Don't treat your cheese like peanut butter by mashing it or spreading it. Just lay it on the bread so you can taste it as a discrete entity.

★ To appreciate cheese at its best, buy little and often. But if you need to store cheese, don't freeze it, suffocate it in plastic wrap, or expose it to strong light or temperature fluctuations.

★ Consider storage places other than the harsh environment of the refrigerator, such as a cellar, garage, or shed—as long as the temperature is moderate (anywhere from 45° to 60°F), the humidity is high enough (ideally 80 percent or more), and there is no exposure to sunlight.

★ If you must store cheese in the refrigerator, use the vegetable drawer, which contains more moisture (especially when there are vegetables in there) than the rest of the refrigerator.

★ For short-term storage: Instead of wrapping the cheese tightly in heavy plastic wrap, cover the cut surface of hard or semi-hard cheese with a light plastic wrap and leave the rind exposed so the cheese can breathe.

★ For soft cheese (with washed or blooming rinds), wrap snugly (but not too tightly) in a lightly waxed, greaseproof paper. Then, on top of that, wrap in light plastic cling-wrap to create an air pocket so the cheese won't suffocate overnight. Change wrappings every day.

Kathy CASEY

★ ★ ★ ★ ★

PROFILE

Kathy Casey has channeled her no-nonsense approach to cooking into a niche market with the establishment of Kathy Casey Food Studios. Located in the heart of Seattle, Casey's namesake 6,000-square-foot studio specializes in food, beverage, and concept development and serves as a location for many of the city's special events. Casey, credited with elevating the reputation of Northwest cuisine to a national level, is the author of *Pacific Northwest: The Beautiful Cookbook*, an IACP Cookbook Award nominee, and writes a monthly food column for the *Seattle Times*.

HOW TO PEEL GINGER WITH A TEASPOON

★ ★ ★ ★ ★ ★ ★ ★ ★ ★ ★

While living in New York, I worked with some great cooks, and of course we would trade chef-to-chef culinary secrets. Well, necessity breeds the greatest inventions and one of the tricks I learned was how to peel a piece of ginger with an ordinary teaspoon. Even though it seems like a simple thing, this technique enabled me to maintain the speed and efficiency necessary on the line in the restaurant. Here's how to do it.

STEP ONE: Take a piece of ginger in one hand and a regular flatware teaspoon (the very same kind you use to stir your coffee) in the other.

STEP TWO: Grip the base of the spoon's bowl between your thumb and fingers and graze the edge down the side of the ginger. Scrape just deep enough to remove the brown skin layer. This method is super-quick for removing just the thin peel and works wonderfully for getting in and around the knobs of the ginger root, wasting much less than if you peel it with a knife.

STEP THREE: If mincing the ginger, cut it lengthwise into thin julienne strips, then very finely cut crosswise to eliminate any stringy fibers. If you chop up more than you need for your recipe, just pop the leftover ginger into a snack-size ziplock bag, press out the air, seal, and freeze for a future use.

MORE CHEF'S SECRETS . . .

FM: What makes Northwest cuisine unique?
KC: Northwest cuisine is not necessarily a dish; it's an attitude inspired by the wonderful local products grown here. The results are flavors that pop and dishes that are bright and fresh.

FM: What's your favorite food indulgence?
KC: My favorite food indulgence is raspberries, fitted on all the tips of my fingers so I can eat them off. I loved doing this when I was a little kid and I still do.

FM: What's your favorite food scene from a movie?
KC: I love the absolutely crazy scene in *Mermaids* where Cher's character dishes up a dinner that consists of a meal on frilly picks. It's like a cocktail party that never ends.

Matthew & Todd BIRNBAUM

★ ★ ★ ★ ★ ★

HOW TO GET A CRISPY PIZZA CRUST AND TENDER TOPPINGS

★ ★ ★ ★ ★ ★ ★ ★ ★ ★ ★ ★

Pizza home cooking challenge: Will the cheese melt in the same time as it takes to heat the sauce and cook the crust? To avoid the issue, cook your crust first with a little sauce in a very hot oven, rest it, and then cook it again in a cooler oven to finish, avoiding the compromises and pitfalls in one fell swoop. While the origin of twice-cooked pizza is Rome, my brother Todd and I first saw this done in Uruguay, specifically the beach resort Punta del Este, where cafés serving *pizza al metro* (pizza by the meter) commonly stay open all night. You can see the long narrow planks of cooling crust lined up and waiting as you enter, and then see your portion cut, topped, and cooked to order.

We loved everything about pizza in this style—from the look to how twice-cooking melted the cheese fresh, charred the crust just a little, and warmed the toppings perfectly. We knew we wanted to bring it to New York—where nobody knows what a meter is. It didn't take long before Todd's joke of a name lodged in everybody's head, and Pinch—Pizza by the Inch—was born.

STEP ONE: Begin with a lightly floured work surface and a ball of dough that's been proofed. (This means dough made with yeast that has risen.)

Using a rolling pin or the heel on your hand, flatten the ball into a disc. (This is called "punching it down.")

STEP TWO: Adapt your rolling pin to fit the size of the pizza. In order to roll the dough out into an even circular shape (a 12-inch diameter, about the size of a record, works well for a small pizza and the home oven), you want to adapt your rolling pin. Take ten thick rubber bands and place five (one on top of another) on each end of your rolling pin. Now your rolling pin is five rubber bands above the surface of the dough. This is like putting tires on your rolling pin and ensures a uniform roll.

STEP THREE: Roll out the dough.

STEP FOUR: Using the back of a wooden spoon, spread on a thin layer of sauce, and bake the dough on an oiled sheet or pizza stone at 500°F until golden brown. After about 3 minutes, begin peeking into the oven.

STEP FIVE: Once the crust is golden, remove the crust from the oven. Let it cool for about 5 minutes, and then top it with your choice of pre-cooked toppings.

STEP SIX: Place the pizza back in the oven at 350°F and cook for about 5 minutes more, until the cheese is melted or you see steam rising from your toppings.

MORE CHEF'S SECRETS . . .

FM: How many inches of pizza can you eat?
MB & TB: Each of us can put away 18 inches of pizza if we are really hungry, and probably nibble more than that just tasting all day long.

FM: The best pizza topping ever?
MB & TB: If we are talking about cheese pizza, then fresh torn basil leaf is the best topping. If we are talking about naked crust, then mozzarella is the answer.

FM: Pizza for breakfast: cold or reheated?
MB & TB: Neither. Leave it out overnight and eat it at room temperature. Putting it in the fridge kills the taste, and heating pizza for breakfast is just wrong.

Jean-Philippe IBERTI & Todd CARMICHAEL

★ ★ ★ ★ ★ ★ ★ ★ ★

PROFILE

Jean-Philippe Iberti and Todd Carmichael, who met in college in Seattle, are partners in the coffee company La Colombe Torrefaction. They started their café-cum-roasting business in 1994 using a 15-kilo Vittoria roaster, and their Philadelphia-based factory now turns out 470 metric tons of roasted coffee beans a year. The original café features a solid wood turn-of-the-century bar, converted into a customized coffee station that accommodates 12 to 14 espresso drinkers (shoulder to shoulder) and serves 1,200 to 1,500 people a day. The master roasters also sell their coffee to some of the country's pickiest chefs, such as Daniel Boulud, Alain Ducasse, and Jean-Georges Vongerichten.

HOW TO MAKE CAPPUCCINO AT HOME

★ ★ ★ ★ ★ ★ ★ ★ ★ ★ ★ ★

You can make a surprisingly silky-smooth cappuccino without an espresso machine. In fact, if you do have an espresso machine, turn it off. All that's required is a small saucepan, two French press coffee makers (a beaker-shaped glass container with metal fittings and a fine wire-mesh plunger), about 2 cups of milk, and some coarse-ground fresh coffee beans. Here's how to make a cappuccino so good that you might consider instituting a tip jar, prominently displayed within view of your guests. (A useful coffee shop trick is to "prime the jar" by adding change and a few small bills to it since no one likes to tip an empty jar.)

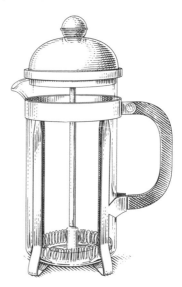

STEP ONE: Use one of the French press makers to prepare the coffee.

STEP TWO: Pour 2 cups of warmed milk into the second French press.

STEP THREE: Insert the plunger into the warmed milk and slowly pump the plunger (sort of like a bicycle tire pump) ten or so times until the milk foams.

STEP FOUR: Pour the coffee into a large cup until it's about one-third full, and then fill to the top with the foamy milk. The milk will be so smooth, you can just pour it in; there is no need to use a spoon.

MORE CHEF'S SECRETS . . .

FM: Personal food fetish?

JPI & TC: Thank God for coffee. It's our life, and this company does not function until we've each had two double espressos.

FM: Favorite movie scene set in a coffee house?

JPI & TC: It's not a coffee house, but in M. Night Shyamalan's *The Sixth Sense*, set in our home base of Philadelphia, when Bruce Willis is sitting in the restaurant Striped Bass, that's a cup of La Colombe coffee in his hands.

FM: Worst coffee trend?

JPI & TC: The fully automated espresso machine used by the coffee superstores breaks our hearts.

COFFEE TIPS FROM JEAN-PHILIPPE IBERTI & TODD CARMICHAEL

★ When making French press coffee, never bring the water to a boil; rather, heat the water to nearly boiling. Boiling water will "scorch" the coffee.

★ For a fuller taste, let the coffee steep in the French press for 2 to 4 minutes before plunging.

★ Make sure your coffee is fresh before you buy it, and purchase only a week's worth at a time. Keep your coffee in a cool, dry place, away from sunlight and odors (with your cups, for example, and not with your spices). Do not put coffee in the refrigerator or freezer—freezing coffee destroys the oils.

HOW TO MAKE A
FLAWLESS OMELET

Lisa
SCHROEDER

★　★　★　★　★　★　★　★　★　★　★　★

I learned how to make a perfect omelet while working at Le Cirque in New York City. Although the only time omelets were on the menu was during restaurant week (when Le Cirque lowered its prix fixe lunch price to $19.95), they still had to be perfect every time. My sous chef, Remy Lauvand, once told me that omelets shouldn't be "wrinkly like my grandmother's underwear." Here's the way we did it.

STEP ONE: Preheat the broiler.

STEP TWO: In a mixing bowl, whisk together 3 eggs with a wire whisk. Set aside.

STEP THREE: Lightly coat the bottom of a new or pristine 8-inch nonstick oven-proof pan with melted clarified butter, swirling to distribute the butter evenly. Pour out any excess butter (if there is too much butter on the bottom of the pan, the omelet will have pockmarks and wrinkles, like the dreaded grandmother's underwear). Clarified butter is ideal when making eggs— because the milk solids are removed, the butter does not brown, lessening the chances that the omelet will brown as well. If clarified butter is not available, use unsalted butter. However, the whole butter will turn brown as it gets hotter, which may cause the omelet to have brown spots or specks—a true no-no.

PROFILE

With over twenty years' experience in the food and restaurant business, Lisa Schroeder is as passionate about pot roast as she is about foie gras. A graduate of the Culinary Institute of America, Schroeder served as an apprentice to French superstars Roger Vergé and Marc Veyrat and also as a line cook at New York's Le Cirque and Lespinasse. As the chef/owner of Mother's Bistro & Bar in Portland, Oregon, Schroeder showcases many different ethnic "Mama-cuisines," promoting her belief that slow-cooked, home-style dishes are some of the most satisfying.

STEP FOUR: Place the pan over medium-high heat (medium heat if using whole butter). Pour in the whisked eggs and use a heat-resistant rubber spatula to stir the eggs as they cook, holding and swirling the pan with your left hand while stirring with the spatula in your right hand.

STEP FIVE: Once the eggs look like they are setting, stop stirring. Push down the edges of the omelet with the spatula to make sure they are even with the bottom of the pan, remove the pan from the heat, and immediately place it under the preheated broiler for about 2 minutes, or until the eggs are set. Be sure to remove the pan from the burner as soon as the eggs start to set or the bottom will quickly turn brown. **Option:** If using a filling, instead of cooking the omelet under the broiler for two minutes, flash it under the broiler for 30 to 60 seconds, just long enough to lightly dry the surface of the eggs (the top should look like it is just about to set). Place filling ingredients in the center of the eggs. Once again, put the pan under the broiler, cooking until the filling is warmed, the cheese (if using) is melted, and the eggs are set to your preferred doneness.

STEP SIX: Grasping the pan with your left hand, tilt it over a serving plate, using the rubber spatula to help fold the omelet, and serve.

MORE CHEF'S SECRETS . . .

FM: What should every mother know how to make?

LS: The common thread of motherhood is woven through many dishes around the world, but there is one dish that nearly every mother in every country makes: chicken soup. Greek mothers make *avgolemono* soup (chicken soup with lemon and rice), Italian mothers have their *stracciatella* (chicken soup with eggs and cheese), Chinese mothers may prepare egg drop or wonton soup, and Jewish mothers are known for their matzoh ball soup.

FM: Favorite cookbook?

LS: My two most favorite cookbooks are the NEW *Joy of Cooking* and Craig Claiborne's *New York Times Cookbook*. They are virtual encyclopedias with accurate, tested recipes, so when directions are followed, the results are typically fabulous.

FM: Treasured kitchen tool?

LS: My favorite kitchen tool is my hands. I use them to mix salads, measure ingredients, and make dough. Nothing works better than my hands when I'm folding egg whites into a cake batter.

W. Park KERR

PROFILE

A ninth-generation Texan, Park Kerr grew up in El Paso on the U.S.-Mexico border and has known and loved chiles all his life. He and his mother, Norma Kerr, started the El Paso Chile Company in 1980, selling dried chile wreaths and *ristras*. An artisan salsa called Salsa Primera became the foundation of today's multi-million dollar business, which now includes several separate labels with a total of more than eighty specialty items. Kerr is also the author of many books, including *The El Paso Chile Company's Texas Border Cookbook*; *The El Paso Chile Company's Burning Desires* (both of which made national best-seller lists); *Beans; Chiles; Tortillas; Sizzlin' Suppers; The El Paso Chile Company Margarita Cookbook*; and *Viva Margarita*.

HOW TO FOLD A BURRITO

★ ★ ★ ★ ★ ★ ★ ★ ★ ★ ★ ★

In the beginning, there was the burrito—the humble bean burrito. But the burrito has now become the cross-cultural "wrap." I remember when the only choice was flour or corn with or without cheese, and to this day I find the most perfect food pairing to be a bean burrito and an Orange Crush. However, you don't just wrap ingredients in a tortilla and call it a burrito—you have to fold, tuck, and roll to get the right leakproof package so you don't end up with burrito in your lap.

STEP ONE: Start with supple, fresh tortillas. In a tortilla emergency, place them in a ziplock bag and microwave them for a couple of seconds to bring them back to life.

STEP TWO: Evenly spread the filling—beans, scrambled eggs, whatever—in the middle of the tortilla, leaving a 2- or 3-inch border all around.

STEP THREE: Sprinkle on the toppings directly over the filling—salsa, cheese, etc.

STEP FOUR: Fold up the bottom of the tortilla about an inch over the filling, tuck the edge of the flap into the filling and wrap it on up into a leakproof package (figures A–D). I like to wrap my burrito in foil and leave it on the dashboard of my car, where it heats up in the west Texas sun. But everybody knows that one—it's sort of a white trash microwave.

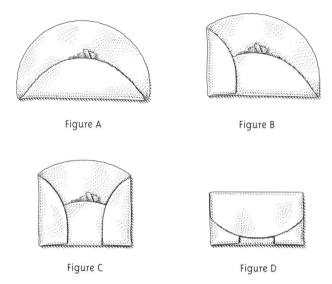

Figure A   Figure B

Figure C   Figure D

MORE CHEF'S SECRETS . . .

FM: The perfect margarita?
WPK: The margarita isn't a drink; it's a lifestyle. Here's how you make it: 1 ounce silver tequila, 1 ounce cheap triple sec, 1 ounce fresh lime juice, and the secret to perfection—a dash of fresh-squeezed orange juice. Shake like hell; serve up.

FM: Best food market?
WPK: The markets that most inspired my life and work are the markets in Juarez, Mexico, where, since I was a small child, I would go to buy and see and eat and smell. The Juarez markets turned me on for life.

FM: Favorite hometown dish?
WPK: Hands down, in the winter, red chile flat enchiladas topped with a fried egg. In any other season, rolled green chile chicken enchiladas with extra sour cream.

Marcus SAMUELSSON

HOW TO CHECK A CURE SOLUTION

★ ★ ★ ★ ★ ★ ★ ★ ★ ★ ★ ★

To properly cure fish or meat, you must have the right mix of water and salt. The way I determine that ratio is with the "egg test," a trick I learned from my Swedish grandmother. Since the amount of the brining solution you need depends on the size of what you are curing, it is best to test the ratio quart by quart.

STEP ONE: Fill a bowl with 1 quart of cool water.

STEP TWO: Add a whole, uncooked egg in the shell (with no cracks).

STEP THREE: Bit by bit, add coarse salt until the egg floats to the surface. When the egg

floats to the top, the brine is salty enough to cure the meat or fish. If the egg stays at the bottom, then you have to add more salt.

MORE CHEF'S SECRETS . . .

FM: If you weren't cooking, what would you be doing?
MS: I'd probably be an artist.

FM: Is there one thing that distinguishes Scandinavian food from other cuisine?
MS: There is such a great play between salt and sugar.

FM: What's your favorite middle-of-the-night food?
MS: I'm not a late-night snacker! The most I enjoy is a glass of cool water.

MARCUS SAMUELSSON'S
SALT-CURED DUCK BREASTS

2 quarts warm water
1 cup coarse salt
4 boneless skin-on duck breasts (about 6 ounces each)

Combine the water and salt in a large bowl, stirring until most of the salt has dissolved. Let cool.

Meanwhile, trim away any excess fat from the duck breasts. Pierce the skin all over with a sharp kitchen fork.

Put the duck breasts into the brine and place a small plate on top of the duck to keep it submerged. Cover and refrigerate for 6 hours.

Preheat the oven to 400°F.

Heat a cast iron skillet over medium heat until hot. Remove the duck breasts from the brine and pat dry with paper towels. Lay the duck breasts skin-side down in the pan and cook for 6 minutes, or until the skin is crisp and browned. Drain most of the fat from the skillet, turn the breasts over, and transfer the skillet to the oven. Roast for 5 minutes. Remove the skillet from the oven and let the duck breasts sit in the hot skillet for 4 minutes to finish cooking.

Thinly slice each duck breast on the diagonal and serve on a bed of salad greens.

HOW TO REMOVE THE WORMS FROM MOREL MUSHROOMS

★ ★ ★ ★ ★ ★ ★ ★ ★ ★ ★ ★ ★

Morels, wild mushrooms found primarily in Oregon, can be up to 3 inches in diameter and are hollow in the middle, making them perfect for stuffing with foie gras or just about anything else. During their mid-spring to mid-summer season, morels grow close to trees in damp conditions. The surface of the mushroom is filled with little crevices where worms (tiny little white strands generally about $1/4$-inch long) can hide. Some chefs soak the morels in salt water to force the worms out, but this can ruin the consistency of the mushroom. Another method is just cutting open the mushroom and removing them by hand, but then you're not left with a whole, intact morel. I know of an easier way that works without fail—here's how to do it.

STEP ONE: Place the morels in a ziplock bag and seal it.

STEP TWO: Leave the bag on the counter. After 2 or 3 hours, all the worms crawl out and stick to the sides of the bag. Without a supply of oxygen, the worms begin to crawl out of the mushrooms and go looking for air. They don't do so on the way to the restaurant because the morels are sent in boxes with holes in the sides, which allows air in and lets the worms remain in the mushrooms.

STEP THREE: Remove the mushrooms—without even touching the worms. You can leave the

Andrew CARTHY

★ ★ ★ ★ ★ ★ ★ ★

PROFILE
Andrew Carthy grew up working on his family's farm in Wexford, Ireland, before attending university and winning a lottery pick in the Morrison visa program that granted him a three-year visa to travel to the United States. His first (and as it turned out, his only) stop was Cape May, New Jersey. Carthy walked into a clothing store on Main Street, asked where he might find work, and was pointed down the street to the Virginia Hotel. After working as a dishwasher and then a valet, he talked his way into a position as a line cook in the hotel's restaurant, the Ebbitt Room, despite no formal training or experience. Now executive chef, Carthy has guided the Ebbitt Room to many awards, including Best of the Best, Best Hotel Dining Room, and Best Romantic Dining from *New Jersey Monthly*.

morels in the bag overnight, but not longer than 12 to 18 hours, because the mushroom will start to give off its own moisture and break down.

MORE CHEF'S SECRETS . . .

FM: What's the difference between a pub and a bar?

AC: A pub, short for public house, is usually divided into two rooms, one being a lounge (where the women generally prefer to drink), and the other a bar, which is usually smaller, with just a counter and stools. My friend's bar back home is classic—old guys talking about days gone by, drinking large bottles of Guinness and "half ones" (a small pour of whiskey, usually served with water).

FM: What's the first thing you do when you get to work?

AC: Get a cup of coffee and yell at somebody.

FM: What's your favorite restaurant (other than your own)?

AC: In New York, Gramercy Tavern. In Cape May, it's Louisa's.

HOW TO DO YOUR OWN STOVE TOP SMOKING

Alison AWERBUCH

★ ★ ★ ★ ★ ★ ★ ★ ★ ★ ★ ★

Smoking is a wonderful way to impart flavor to a variety of different foods, even unlikely suspects like cheese and fruit. This process of stove top smoking is quick and easy and can be done well in advance of serving. Create an entire dish out of smoked ingredients, or just use a few as a subtle complement. You can also drizzle a finishing glaze on the food before serving, using balsamic vinegar, infused olive oil, honey, pesto, or chili oil. Here's how you can saturate foods with smoked flavor right on your stove top.

STEP ONE: Soak 4 cups of wood chips in warm water for 1 hour. Wood chips—from distinctively smoky, bacon-like hickory, earthy mesquite, or mildly sweet apple—are available at hardware stores or gourmet markets; choose the type that best suits your taste. See page 43 for suggestions on the amount. Make sure the chips are completely immersed in the water.

STEP TWO: Place the soaked wood chips in a durable, industrial-weight 11 x 14-inch heavy-bottomed roasting or baking pan. Scatter aromatics (see list of suggested peelings, spices, herbs, and liquid flavorings on page 43) and 1 cup of water over the wood chips.

STEP THREE: Place a wire-mesh baking rack (sprayed with cooking oil) over the wood chips.

PROFILE

Alison Awerbuch, who trained at the Culinary Institute of America, oversees the food and beverage operations for Abigail Kirsch Culinary Productions, one of Manhattan's premier caterers. As partner and chief culinary officer, Awerbuch is responsible for producing more than one thousand events each year for clients such as Tiffany, Tommy Hilfiger, and the Big Apple Circus as well as five hundred weddings annually. She is also vice president of Les Dames d'Escoffier New York, a culinary and mentoring organization.

STEP FOUR: Place a lid over the roasting pan and put it on a stove top burner set on the lowest heat. Make sure the pan is covered tightly so no air can escape. (If you don't have a lid, use an empty stockpot to weight down a cookie sheet.) If your roasting pan is large, it may need to be placed on two burners side by side. Heat over low heat for 20 minutes, until the wood starts to smolder and smoke.

STEP FIVE: Uncover your makeshift smoker and place the selected ingredients on the wire rack. Cover tightly, and let cook until smoked and tender. For a list of items I recommend smoking, see page 43. Softer vegetables will take about 20 minutes, harder vegetables and fruits about 30 minutes—test for doneness by making sure they are fork tender. Cheeses will take about 10 minutes.

STEP SIX: Turn off the burners and leave the covered pan on the stove for an additional 10 minutes to continue the smoking and cooking process. After 10 minutes, uncover the pan. Serve the food, or let it cool and refrigerate.

MORE CHEF'S SECRETS . . .

FM: Food person ahead of his or her time?
AA: Alice Waters, one of the first chefs to promote (in a big way) the sustainable food movement and local farmers, is a culinarian who is a visionary.

FM: Favorite cookbook?
AA: I love reference cookbooks and one of my favorites is the Culinary Institute of America's *The Professional Chef*. Whenever I need to refresh myself on the proper technique, cooking methods, or ingredients/recipes for classic dishes, this is what I refer to.

FM: Biggest mistake a home cook can make when entertaining?
AA: Planning a menu that is too complicated. Your guests have a much better time when you are out of the kitchen, relaxing with a glass of wine and having a good time—not when you are the invisible host who is stuck in the kitchen all night.

AROMATICS TO ENHANCE
THE SMOKED FLAVOR

Fruit Peelings, $1/2$ cup
★ Apple
★ Pear
★ Orange
★ Grapefruit
★ Lemon
★ Lime
★ Pineapple

Fresh Hearty Herbs, 1 bunch
★ Rosemary
★ Thyme
★ Savory
★ Lavender
★ Sage

Spices, $1/2$ cup
★ Chopped fresh ginger
★ Cinnamon sticks
★ Star anise
★ Juniper berries
★ Cloves
★ Lemongrass
★ Peppercorns

Liquid Flavorings, $3/4$ cup
★ Sesame oil
★ Orange juice
★ Lemon juice
★ Apple juice
★ Pear nectar
★ Maple syrup
★ Rice wine vinegar

INGREDIENTS FOR SMOKING

Vegetables, in 1-inch-thick slices
★ Portobello mushroom caps
★ Fennel bulbs, cut in sixths
★ Carrots, peeled
★ Potatoes or yams, blanched

Cheese, in 1-inch-thick slices, wrapped in fig or banana leaves
★ Feta
★ Kasseri (Greek sheep-milk cheese)
★ Aged provolone

Fruit
★ Pineapples with the rind off, sliced 1 inch thick
★ Pears, cored and cut in 1-inch wedges
★ Oranges with the rind on, cut in $3/4$-inch-thick slices
★ Lemons with the rind on, cut in $3/4$-inch-thick slices
★ Whole bananas left in the skin
★ Whole fresh figs

CHAPTER TWO
★ ★ ★ ★
MEAT & POULTRY

Jim GALLE

HOW TO DEFROST MEAT, POULTRY, AND GAME

★ ★ ★ ★ ★ ★ ★ ★ ★ ★ ★ ★

Growing up, part of my Thanksgiving tradition was seeing our holiday turkey in the sink bobbing around in that tepid water like a fishing cork. We all survived that bacteria minefield so it must be a good way to defrost or "slack out" our proteins correctly—*not!* Even in top kitchens that demand the freshest product, meats, poultry, and game occasionally find their way to the freezer. What is the best way to bring these often expensive cuts back to a state of appealing quality? It is quite simple, but the keys are planning and patience. With this method, very little liquid will purge from the product. (Very little "purge" means a moist and tender finished product; lots of "purge" means drier and tougher.)

STEP ONE: Figure out how much time you will need. Decide when you need the product ready. Generally speaking, give your product 1 to 2 days to come up in temperature from frozen solid to well-chilled but totally defrosted. Remember that size and density come into play when deciding how much time you need.

STEP TWO: Defrost in the refrigerator. In professional kitchens, they know that you want the product to slack out (defrost) in a very cold and well-circulated environment. Unless you have commercial-quality walk-in coolers in your apartment, the refrigerator is your only very cold, well-circulated environment. Simply clear out some space on a middle rack and slide your loosely wrapped meat in the fridge. Put a drip pan below to catch any liquids that may fall away. If space is tight, just put the meat in the drip pan. Over the next day or two, when you gently touch the meat, you will feel the "springiness" coming back.

MORE CHEF'S SECRETS . . .

FM: What's your favorite bar snack?
JG: Real Tex-Mex chili con queso with chips.

FM: Is there any politically correct way to order a steak well-done?
JG: At a drive-through window in the form of a 99-cent cheeseburger. Seriously, if you pay for it, you should get it how you like it. No one is more correct than anyone else when it comes to taste in food and wine.

FM: There's a sign on your office door: What does it read?
JG: What do you expect? J. Galle, Vice President, Grimaud Farms.

Robert PEARSON

HOW TO BARBECUE TENDER MEAT

★ ★ ★ ★ ★ ★ ★ ★ ★ ★ ★

After all the meat I've cooked in my life, it comes down to this: Meat should not be cooked above an internal temperature of 212°F, the boiling point of water. Cooking above 212°F basically boils the internal juices, rendering the meat too dry. No matter what cut of meat you are cooking, insert an internal thermometer and check it hourly. It should register between 208° and 212°F and never go above that internal temperature. This is not such an issue when you are cooking a small cut of meat like chops or steak, or a roast that you want to serve rare to medium rare (since the internal temperature will not rise above 135°F or so). But when you are slow cooking a large cut of beef, something like brisket or pot roast (meat served extremely well done), it is essential.

STEP ONE: Start with room temperature meat. Let's pretend that you are barbecuing a 10-pound brisket. First, make sure that the meat is at room temperature and not fridge temperature, so you won't waste cooking time trying to bring up its temperature and dry the meat further.

STEP TWO: Barbecue over wood or lump charcoal. As a heat source, wood is better than charcoal, but if you're using charcoal, don't allow the fat to drip on it—arrange the hot coals on either side of the meat and set a pan directly under the brisket to catch the dripping juices.

STEP THREE: Cook at 175°F for about 1 hour per pound of meat, checking the internal temperature hourly. Brisket is done when you pick it up at one end and it feels like it will break off. Once done, allow the brisket to rest, and then start slicing (on the diagonal) from the thin end.

MORE CHEF'S SECRETS . . .

FM: Biggest misconception about barbecue?
RP: People think that barbecue is cooked by the smoke in the pit. But in fact, it's the heat that rises from the wood.

FM: Who's your food hero?
RP: Louie Mueller of Louie Mueller's in Taylor, Texas—one of the all-time great pit men.

FM: Best bar snack ever?
RP: I'll stick with peanuts.

James CANNON

HOW TO CHOOSE PRIME BEEF

★ ★ ★ ★ ★ ★ ★ ★ ★ ★ ★ ★

One critical lesson I've learned over the years in the kitchen is to always use USDA Prime beef. With all the different grades of beef available—Prime, Choice, Select, and No Roll (or not officially graded)—the average consumer is confused when trying to determine the highest quality cut of meat. Here are some important tips to follow when selecting and preparing a high-grade piece of Prime beef.

★ **Don't be fooled—fat is your friend.** Be sure to select a piece of meat that's well marbled with ribbons of fat. A piece of lean meat may look appetizing and better for the waistline, but the steak will turn out tough no matter how you cook it. A little fat enhances the flavor and texture of the meat.

★ **Color is key.** The natural red color of fresh meat may be a very appealing sight, but it's not as much of an appealing taste. When you're at the local supermarket or butcher shop, select a piece of beef that has more of a reddish brown than a bright red color, which means the beef has been exposed to oxygen and will have a superior flavor.

★ **Have patience, my friend, patience.** Carnivores are usually anxious to devour their beautifully marbled Prime steak as soon as humanly possible, but it is important to take note of this step in order to have the ultimate steak experience. Prior to cooking your steak, let the meat sit for 30 to 35 minutes until it reaches room temperature. This allows the meat to tenderize naturally and will improve its taste, texture, and receptiveness to seasoning.

MORE CHEF'S SECRETS . . .

FM: What is the advice you give people on their first day in your kitchen?
JC: To listen and watch. And to make sure none of their fingers leave their hand.

FM: Any acceptable way to order a steak well-done?
JC: If you are to order well-done, make sure the steak will not be butterflied (split open). Well-done is not the best way to eat a steak, but if it is not butterflied, it will still have some juice.

FM: What kind of steak would you put on a black eye?
JC: None! Why waste a good steak? Ice works much better!

PRIME TIPS FROM JAMES CANNON

★ **Seasoning:** If you choose to season your meat, use a little salt, pepper, and olive oil. Don't mask the natural taste of your Prime steak with fancy seasonings or marinades. You'll be missing out on the reason you splurged on Prime beef!

★ **Temperature:** Before you start cooking, crank up the oven, or if you're cooking out, make sure the charcoals are white hot—the higher the temperature, the better. The heat will lock in the steak's natural flavors and juices. But keep a close watch so as not to overcook the meat.

★ **The Touch Test:** The key to test how a steak is cooked is by touch— the softer the meat, the less cooked it is.

★ **The Magic of Butter:** One more trick to enhance the flavor of your Prime steak is to add a little butter to the mix. It may be more fattening, but it tenderizes and brings out the natural flavors of the meat. Your steak will melt in your mouth "like buuddaaah!"

HOW TO FORM
A BURGER PATTY

★ ★ ★ ★ ★ ★ ★ ★ ★ ★ ★ ★ ★

The meat you use to make a burger needs to be fresh and free of excessive moisture. If you shop at a supermarket (instead of a butcher), the meat should not have any excess blood in the package. The color should be sharp, not faded or brown. If using frozen meat, thaw the meat overnight in the refrigerator. Do not run it under water or let it stand at room temperature. The two most important points in forming a burger patty are (1) tightness and (2) shape. Keeping the beef well refrigerated will help you form a tighter patty.

STEP ONE: Season the meat. Place the ground beef in a bowl. If you plan on cooking the burgers immediately, season the meat with salt and freshly ground black pepper and mix very well. However, if the burgers are not going to be cooked within 15 minutes, do not season the beef. (The salt actually starts to cook the beef, drawing out water and thereby curing the meat.)

STEP TWO: Form the meat into balls. Start by tearing portions out of the bowl and forming them loosely into round balls. Then, palm-to-palm, toss the beef balls back and forth. You must be patient with this step—you're looking for a perfect ball; no cracks or crevices. Place the balls on wax paper.

STEP THREE: Flatten the patties. Gently press the meat between your palms, pushing so that the

William Bradford
GATES

★ ★ ★ ★ ★ ★ ★ ★ ★ ★ ★ ★ ★

PROFILE

Born in Indiana, Brad Gates moved to New York City to attend the French Culinary Institute, and after graduating with honors, secured a position under Chef Michael Romano at Union Square Café, where he was promoted to sous chef in 1994. Gates was also *chef de cuisine* at Union Square Café, the winner of the James Beard Awards for Outstanding Service and Restaurant of the Year, and the Zagat Survey's Most Popular Restaurant in New York City. As consulting chef with the Myriad Restaurant Group, he covered Icon, Heartbeat, Earth & Ocean, and Tribeca Grill restaurants before becoming executive chef of Pioneer, where he has developed an exceptional repertoire of seasonal wild game specialties.

top and bottom are flat. The patty should be at least 3/4 inch thick in order to cook evenly. Keep the edges rounded for the same reason. Crimp and tuck the patty to rid it of any newly formed cracks or crevices.

STEP FOUR: Season the outside of the patties. Add salt and pepper. Lightly rub the meat with canola oil and then place the patties between layers of wax paper. Refrigerate until you're ready to cook.

MORE CHEF'S SECRETS . . .

FM: Best food movie ever?
WBG: *Big Night.*

FM: Weirdest piece of kitchen equipment you use?
WBG: Ronco food dehydrator.

FM: Favorite bar food?
WBG: Oysters on the half shell with a Sierra Nevada Pale Ale; it's a beautiful thing.

HOW TO MAKE PORK MORE FLAVORFUL

★ ★ ★ ★ ★ ★ ★ ★ ★ ★ ★ ★

Bruce AIDELLS

This brining technique, which you'll master the first time out, will change the whole way you relate to lean pork. Brining will ensure that you'll never serve a dried-out, hard, tasteless pork chop again, and your pork loin roasts will be juicy and tender. If you serve pork chops, pork loin roasts, or pork tenderloins on a regular basis, why not store some already-made brine in your refrigerator? It keeps for several weeks. There is one caveat: Make sure you don't overcook your pork. A final internal temperature somewhere between 145° and 155°F is what you want.

STEP ONE: Dissolve salt in water. The formula of $^1/_4$ cup table salt to 8 cups water allows for the brining process to be slow and controllable.

STEP TWO: Cool the brine to a temperature of less than 45°F. The temperature of the brine affects the process immensely, especially the diffusion of salt into the meat. Diffusion happens much quicker once the temperature is raised. To be consistent and controllable, all brining should be done at refrigerator temperature, 45°F or lower.

STEP THREE: Put your meat of choice into a ziplock bag, add enough brine to cover it, and then put it in the fridge. The amount of time the meat needs to brine is determined by its size—a large piece of meat, like a roast, takes an overnight soaking, while small pieces, like chops,

PROFILE

Bruce Aidells, a.k.a. "The Sausage King," holds a Ph.D. in biology from the University of California, Santa Cruz. Ultimately, biological research couldn't compete with good food, and Aidells exchanged his lab coat for a chef's toque at Poulet, a popular Berkeley restaurant and charcuterie, before founding Aidells Sausage Company. He has written nine cookbooks, including his latest book, *The Complete Book of Pork; The Complete Meat Cookbook*, which was nominated for a James Beard Award; and *Hot Links and Country Flavors* (both coauthored with Denis Kelly), which both won the IACP Cookbook Award for Best Single-Subject Cookbook. Aidells also contributed the meat and poultry chapters of the revised *Joy of Cooking* as well as the key meat tips in *The All New Good Housekeeping Cookbook*.

take only 3 to 4 hours. Experiment, but be aware that it is possible to over brine, which will cause the meat to become too salty.

STEP FOUR: Remove the meat, pat it dry, and proceed with the recipe. You can refrigerate the meat out of the brine for a day or two or until you're ready to use it.

MORE CHEF'S SECRETS . . .

FM: Best Christmas gift to give your butcher?
BA: *The Complete Meat Cookbook* and a tub of homemade lard.

FM: Favorite junk food?
BA: Carnitas tacos.

FM: Essential kitchen utensil?
BA: Digital instant-read thermometer.

HOW TO CARVE A WHOLE HAM

★ ★ ★ ★ ★ ★ ★ ★ ★ ★ ★ ★

Sharon MEEHAN

I like to serve a whole ham because you get the butt and the shank: The butt is the prettier slicing end, and the shank is the fattier end (with the hock at the end of it). I like the shank end because I love fat on meat, and I also like how a big ol' peppered ham looks on a platter. Since it can be a little messy, start the process in the kitchen, wedging the ham out and then carving from that shank end, working your way down to the butt end. It's easier to carve if you can visualize it, so hold a whole ham up to your butt. Let the butt end be your butt and imagine the shank end going down your leg.

STEP ONE: Remove a wedge from the ham. Using a thin-bladed, flexible carving knife held perpendicular to the shank (narrow end), cut a wedge at a 45-degree angle (Figure A). Remove the wedge and any remaining fat from the top of the ham.

STEP TWO: Move the knife along the contour of the bone. Starting at the wedge, slice straight

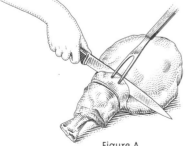

Figure A

PROFILE

Sharon Meehan, president and CEO of Ham I Am!, began her career in the gourmet meat business in 1986 by transporting cracked pepper—encrusted, no-water-added smoked hams from Arkansas to Texas in the back of her white Volkswagen Rabbit and selling them door to door. Since then Meehan has managed to turn Ham I Am! into a million dollar—plus company, with such products as a ham glaze called Hogwash, peppered bacon, red wine brisket, and marinated quail. In addition to select retail stores coast-to-coast, Meehan's products are also sold through some of the country's best mail order catalogs, such as Neiman Marcus and Harry and David.

down from the shank end to the butt end, cutting the meat down to the bone (Figure B). Once you have the meat sliced straight to the bone, it is easy to glide the blade of the knife along the contour of bone and lift the slices right off.

STEP THREE: Take the remaining ham back into the kitchen, flip it over, and carve the underside lengthwise into long, thin slices (Figure C).

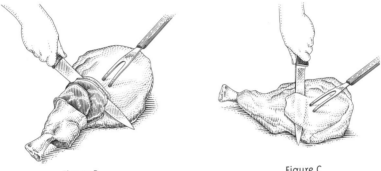

Figure B   Figure C

MORE CHEF'S SECRETS . . .

FM: You started your company by selling hams door-to-door. What was your opening line?
SM: "Do you want to taste a ham that tastes the way ham used to taste?"

FM: Someone once said that eternity is two people and a ham. What do you do with your leftovers?
SM: Black bean soup made with the ham bone, topped with sour cream and chopped scallions, served with cornbread—lots of butter on the cornbread.

FM: Favorite beverage cure for ham's saltiness?
SM: Our ham is not salty—true story!

HOW TO BONE
A LEG OF LAMB

★ ★ ★ ★ ★ ★ ★ ★ ★ ★ ★ ★

Lamb is an important and popular Greek food. In fact, at Molyvos, we should have a metered sign that says, "Over 4 billion served" and keeps counting. I roast so many legs of lamb that I've discovered how to get a better "grip" on the situation by only partially boning them.

STEP ONE: Remove the top of the flesh from the bone. Lay the lamb on the cutting board, fat side up. Run your knife around the top part of the shank (Figure A), just to separate and remove the top 2 inches of flesh from the bone (the shank runs deep into the flesh). This technique is known as frenching.

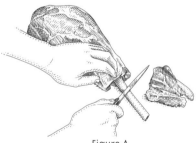

Figure A

STEP TWO: Separate the femur (thigh bone) from the shank bone. Grasp the shank and apply a small amount of pressure; the meat will bend at the joint. Make a small incision at the joint (Figure B). Insert the point of a filet knife or a stiff boning knife into the incision.

James
BOTSACOS

★ ★ ★ ★ ★ ★ ★

PROFILE

A descendant of talented Greek- and Italian-American chefs, James Botsacos began his cooking career in high school with a three-week apprenticeship at Johnson and Wales University in Rhode Island. He later earned a degree from the school's two-year study program. Botsacos, former sous chef at New York's 21 Club, was executive chef at Park Avalon and consulting chef at Blue Water Grill before taking over the kitchen at Molyvos. He traveled to Greece, where he met with Greek food authority Aglaia Kremezi to research the country's regional home cooking. In 1997, he received a three-star review from the *New York Times*. That same year, *Esquire* named Molyvos among the Best in America.

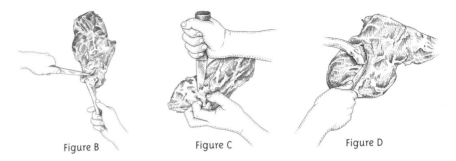

Figure B   Figure C   Figure D

STEP THREE: Turn the leg over, fat-side down. Using your fingers, follow the bone down the center of the leg. Grasp the knife handle with your fist (like you're ready to stab something) and run the tip of the knife on top of the bone along the full length of the meat. Along one side, run the knife repeatedly along the length of the bone, pulling the meat away as you go (Figure C). Repeat this process on the other side so that the only meat attached to the bone is underneath it. Now the bone is fully exposed.

STEP FOUR: Remove the bone. Insert your knife underneath the bone and run it up and down the length of the bone to separate it from the underside of the meat (Figure D). The bone will easily come out in your hand, and you still have a part of the shank attached, which makes the leg of lamb easier to carve and prettier to serve.

MORE CHEF'S SECRETS . . .

FM: What do you serve a finicky eater?
JB: Familiar ingredients—something plain grilled, not highly seasoned or garnished, maybe a little olive oil and lemon.

FM: Name an ingredient you can't live without.
JB: Garlic! I'll eat it any way: whole roasted, raw puréed, toasted into chips.

FM: What's your favorite restaurant other than your own?
JB: Blue Ribbon, New York City.

HOW TO JOINT
A CHICKEN

★ ★ ★ ★ ★ ★ ★ ★ ★ ★ ★ ★

David
WALTUCK

Poultry is the backbone of our staff meals for the same reason it is in other families—it's inexpensive, always available, and highly adaptable. Although supermarkets offer prewrapped chicken pieces, buying a whole chicken and cutting it yourself gives you a fresher-tasting bird. The first thing you need is a good, sharp knife, like a 6-inch boning knife, because of the thin, flexible blade. Cutting a chicken is slippery work, so you'll also need plenty of paper towels to wipe off your hands and the handle of the knife during the process. In the end, you will have eight pieces of chicken—four breast pieces and four leg pieces.

★ **Legs.** First, place the whole chicken (breast-side up) on a clean, dry work surface. Locate the joint that attaches the leg to the body, and cut through it (Figure A). Divide the leg by cutting through the joint that attaches the drumstick to the thigh (Figure B). Do the same thing with the other leg.

Figure A

Figure B

★ **Breast meat.** Work one side of the chicken at a time. Make a cut along one side of the breastbone near the wing end of the chicken (Figure C). Ease the meat off that half of the breast by cutting alongside the rib cage to the tail end. Cut through the joint that attaches the wing to the body (Figure D) and remove the breast meat in one piece.

Remove the tip of the wing; then divide the breast meat in half: One side will be completely boneless, and the other will include the wing. Repeat on the other side.

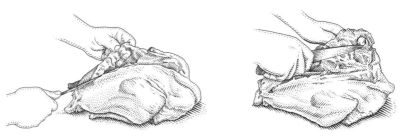

Figure C   Figure D

MORE CHEF'S SECRETS . . .

FM: If your kitchen had a motto, what would it be?
DW: Fat equals flavor.

FM: An anthem?
DW: "(Shake, Shake, Shake), Shake Your Booty" by K.C. & the Sunshine Band.

FM: A mascot?
DW: Elvis!

HOW TO ROAST A CHICKEN—PERFECTLY

★ ★ ★ ★ ★ ★ ★ ★ ★ ★ ★ ★

I learned this trick while traveling in Europe and first employed it when we opened the Red Cat. It's a traditional technique used in the countryside in Spain and Italy. In Italy, it is a peasant-style dish, cooked over an open fire; in Spain, the chicken is cooked on a flat griddle. I sear my chicken in a hot pan and finish cooking it in a preheated oven.

STEP ONE: Preheat the oven to 350°F.

STEP TWO: Start with a boned chicken. To replicate our restaurant portion, start with a half chicken that has been completely boned with the skin left intact. The boning process is tricky and your butcher can do this for you. The boned chicken is easier to eat, and leaving the skin intact helps keep the bird in one piece.

STEP THREE: Wrap a clean brick or rock in foil.

STEP FOUR: Use the wrapped brick to help sear the chicken. Heat a film of olive oil in an oven-proof skillet or shallow roasting pan. A roasting pan is better when you're making multiple dinners simultaneously because it has a larger cooking surface. Season the chicken with salt and pepper and press it skin-side down in the hot pan, using the brick as a weight. Sear until the skin crisps and browns slightly, about 4 minutes. The brick ensures that the chicken will be evenly cooked and evenly crisp.

Jimmy BRADLEY

PROFILE

Fourth-generation Italian-American Jimmy Bradley grew up loving to cook and can remember family meals in vivid detail. His maternal ancestors immigrated to America, establishing the Bartolomeo Pio Wine Company in the 1950s, and his grandmother, the company's winemaker, often hosted gatherings for the company's patrons and employees. These early experiences provided Bradley with a direct connection to his Italian roots and the welcoming and genuine spirit of Old World hospitality. Praised by the *New York Times* for his "easy, natural style," Bradley, a former culinary consultant who traveled through Italy studying cooking and viniculture, stays focused on the same family fundamentals in his three restaurants, the Red Cat, the Harrison, and the Mermaid Inn, all in New York City.

STEP FIVE: Finish by roasting the chicken in the oven. Remove the brick and transfer the pan to a preheated 350°F oven. Your chicken will be perfectly roasted in about 10 minutes.

MORE CHEF'S SECRETS . . .

FM: What was a food idea ahead of its time?

JB: In the late 1800s and early 1900s, dishes such as the carpetbag (steak stuffed with oysters) and steak tartare (raw meat served in a time when everyone else ate it well-done) were both really ahead of their time.

FM: Why does roast chicken continue to be a menu favorite?

JB: I like chicken for its diversity. It is a blank canvas—with both light and dark meat and a high fat content—that picks up all the flavors of its sauce and accoutrements.

FM: What is always in your fridge at home?

JB: Lemons. All I really need to cook is lemon, salt and pepper, and olive oil.

HOW TO ROAST FOWL

★ ★ ★ ★ ★ ★ ★ ★ ★ ★ ★

Charlie PALMER

★ ★ ★ ★ ★ ★ ★ ★

The serious cook should not practice buying anything wrapped in plastic, including fowl. With that said, at least try to buy birds with some type of pedigree (it really is worth the extra dollars), such as hormone-free, free-range, and birds that haven't been exposed to ice-water plunges. Here's how to roast your bird to its best advantage.

STEP ONE: Dry out the bird. Pat it dry with heavy-gauge paper towels, being sure to get around the joints and especially in the cavity. Place it uncovered in the refrigerator overnight.

STEP TWO: Season the bird with herbs, spices, and lemon. The next step is to rub the bird's skin with any type of spice, such as dry oregano, half a garlic clove, and any kind of chili powder, all according to your preference. Next, roll a lemon and cut it in half; rub the entire bird with both halves of the lemon. Place the lemons in the cavity, along with half a clove of garlic (only if you like garlic, of course) and whatever fresh herbs you like, leaving room for airflow.

STEP THREE: Rub the entire bird with very good extra-virgin olive oil. Yes, even rub turkeys with olive oil—you can always add butter later.

STEP FOUR: Season with salt and pepper. Keep in mind that large birds, whether a turkey, duck,

PROFILE

Charlie Palmer worked at the legendary La Côte Basque with Chef Jean-Jacques Rachou and at the River Café before opening Aureole on Manhattan's Upper East Side. Palmer, a James Beard Best Chef Award winner and member of Who's Who in Food & Beverage in America, also owns Métrazur, which overlooks Grand Central Terminal in New York City; Aureole at Mandalay Bay Resort and Casino; Charlie Palmer Steak at the Four Seasons Hotel in Las Vegas; and Dry Creek Kitchen, located in the Palmer-owned Hotel Healdsburg in Sonoma, California. In September 2002 he opened Kitchen 22, an intimate neighborhood restaurant in the Flatiron section of New York City, and he recently opened Kitchen 82, his first restaurant on the Upper West Side. Palmer is also the author of three books, including his latest, *The Art of Aureole*.

or capon, almost always need to be overseasoned. When you baste the bird, you're literally washing away some of the salt. Make sure that you season the inner cavity to the same extent as the outside.

STEP FIVE: Prop the cavity open with a wooden dowel or metal skewer. Opening the bird in this way allows hot air to flow inside the cavity, which reduces cooking time and makes for more even cooking. I also like to drive a skewer into the thick part of the thigh to conduct heat directly into the part that takes the longest time to cook, ensuring the breast meat is not overcooked.

STEP SIX: Roast the bird. Always roast on a well-oiled rack to allow airflow underneath the bird. Convection ovens are ideal for roasting birds—first, at 425°F (calibrate the oven for accuracy) for about 20 minutes and then turn it down to 350°F until it's finished. My rule of thumb with turkeys is 12 to 13 minutes per pound.

STEP SEVEN: Baste with butter and pan drippings. With all the gadgets out there for basting birds, the best is still a stick of sweet butter with the wrapper peeled down from one end to keep your fingers from getting sticky (especially if you're trying to flip back and forth between multiple football games on your Direct TV remote!). The other tool you'll need is a large serving spoon—tilt the pan and spoon the pan drippings all over the bird. Basting with the pan drippings will create "stains" on the otherwise perfectly golden brown skin, but from a taste standpoint, you can't beat it.

STEP EIGHT: Let it rest, carve, and serve. Always let the bird rest before applying a (hopefully) quite sharp carving knife—for a chicken, wait 10 to 15 minutes; for a turkey, wait at least 20 to 25 minutes. Of course, plenty of pinot noir should be on hand to wash down the extremely moist flesh and crispy, slightly salty skin. Cheers!

MORE CHEF'S SECRETS . . .

FM: Most overrated food trend?
CP: Miniscule/precious dishes that are wildly expensive and not filling (leaving you with no choice but to get a slice afterward), causing drunkenness during the wait between courses. I truly believe that people still come to a restaurant to be nourished and satisfied from a hunger standpoint.

FM: Best kitchen advice?
CP: From an old Belgian chef—no matter how many people tell you how great it is to be a star chef, working 14 hours a day, usually in not very healthy conditions (i.e., 95-degree heat, breathing smoke, and standing on your feet on slippery floors), is not that glamorous, and you better really love cooking on a basic level.

FM: What is always in your fridge at home?
CP: Orange juice, mayo (Hellmann's), Dijon mustard, usually a few bottles of white wine and champagne, grape jelly, cream cheese, and a variety of leftovers—in Tupperware.

John VILLA

PROFILE

John Villa's early influences were all centered in food. His grandparents grew their own tomatoes for sauce and made their own pasta; his parents were restaurant adventurers. After graduating from the Culinary Institute of America, Villa settled in New York City, cooking under Daniel Boulud at Le Cirque and under Ed Brown at Judson Grill. At twenty-four, Villa became executive chef of Judson Grill, earning two stars from the *New York Times* as well as a James Beard Foundation nomination for Rising Star Chef. Tapped to reinvigorate the kitchen of the newly remodeled Boathouse at Central Park, he received a three-star *New York Times* review and then another when he opened his Portuguese-influenced Pico. Now executive chef and partner in the venerable Patroon, Villa turns out "brand new classics" that showcase his flair for innovation.

HOW TO ENSURE A CRISP ROAST DUCK

★ ★ ★ ★ ★ ★ ★ ★ ★ ★ ★

Many people are reluctant to order duck because they think it will be too fatty. When they do order it, they don't want to see any fat at all. But there has to be some fat on a duck to keep the meat succulent and tasty. Although this step can seem like a bit of a bother, it will produce just the right balance: rendered fat, crisp skin, moist meat, and lots of flavor.

STEP ONE: Boil water in a large stockpot. Fill a large stockpot with enough water to submerge your duck. Bring the water to a boil. Since the duck is only going to be submerged for a short period of time, the water does not have to be seasoned, although you can certainly do so if you like.

STEP TWO: Dunk the duck in the boiling water. Secure the duck under the wings with a lasso of strong kitchen twine or place a small meat hook in the cavity (but do not pierce the skin). Suspend the duck in the boiling water for about 30 seconds to heat the fat and jump-start the melting process without cooking the duck. If the water stops boiling, the duck has been in the water for too long.

STEP THREE: Allow the duck to dry. Remove the duck and stand it up (cavity-side down) in a colander suspended over another pot or bowl. Let the water and fat drip out. Cover and refrigerate overnight or for up to 2 days.

STEP FOUR: Season the duck. When the duck is dry, season the cavity with coarse salt, black pepper, thyme, and orange zest (do not season the outside of the duck because the salt will cause the skin to shrink and tear). The skin on the duck must be totally dry or the meat will steam in the oven; the drier the skin, the better it will crisp during cooking.

STEP FIVE: Roast the duck according to your favorite recipe.

MORE CHEF'S SECRETS . . .

FM: When you were six, you asked Santa for a Bundt pan. What would you ask for now?
JV: A Ducati would be nice.

FM: Any advice for the next culinary generation?
JV: Never presume you've learned all there is. Keep your eyes and mind open to new techniques and ideas. I'm always learning something from my cooks.

FM: What's your favorite family meal?
JV: Breakfast on Saturday. We get up early and hit the farmers' market before the crowds do. Then we come home and I cook up some pancakes and bacon (which my kids think is the best thing in my repertoire).

CHAPTER THREE

★ ★ ★ ★

FISH & SHELLFISH

Gregory
ZAPANTIS

★ ★ ★ ★ ★ ★ ★ ★ ★ ★

HOW TO DEAL WITH
A WHOLE FISH

★ ★ ★ ★ ★ ★ ★ ★ ★ ★ ★ ★

Whole fish has become not only a very popular menu item in restaurants, but also a popular dish for the home cook. To select the fish, it is important to recognize the qualities that indicate freshness, like bright, clear eyes and a fresh smell; shiny and tightly layering scales; firm flesh (will spring back to shape when pressed); and reddish pink color around the gills. Fish are highly perishable and must be kept under refrigeration at all times. Fresh fish must be kept below 40°F and preferably near 32° to 36°F. Crushed ice is the best refrigerant for fresh fish. It holds the temperature, keeps the fish moist, and most importantly, it allows the fish to hold its natural shape.

STEP ONE: Prepare the fish. If you have purchased your fish from a fishmonger, it is probably scaled, gutted, and cleaned (flat fish should also be skinned). Now the fun begins. For round fish, lay the fish on its side. Using a small, sharp paring knife, make four incisions of medium

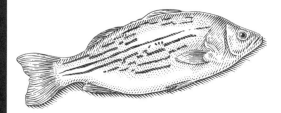

depth between the head and the tail, in the filet. Flip the fish and repeat. (For flat fish, score each side on top and bottom.)

STEP TWO: Marinate the fish. Combine 3 parts olive oil to 1 part lemon juice and add a healthy pinch of coarse salt and coarsely ground back pepper. Rub the entire fish with the marinade and place several sprigs of thyme and oregano inside the cavity of the fish.

STEP THREE: Cook the fish. Once the fish is well bathed in the marinade (about 4 hours), place it in an oven-proof vessel with the remainder of the liquid. Roast at 425°F uncovered for 15 minutes per pound.

MORE CHEF'S SECRETS . . .

FM: Ingredient you can't live without?
GZ: Extra-virgin olive oil.

FM: Best cooking advice you ever got?
GZ: Stick to the basics and do them well.

FM: Most prized kitchen possession?
GZ: Peltex slotted fish spatula, oyster knife, and filet knife.

Denis FITZGERALD

★ ★ ★ ★ ★ ★ ★

PROFILE

Denis Fitzgerald, executive chef at New York's Remi, combines traditional Venetian dishes with modern cooking techniques. Born in New York City, Fitzgerald began his career at the age of fourteen in a family restaurant, working alongside his older brother. He later attended the Culinary Institute of America before working at some of New York City's finest restaurants, including Aureole, Oceana, and Il Cantinori, but the years he spent working at the legendary Lutèce were the most influential of his career. Citing Lutèce's legendary chef/proprietor André Soltner's "extensive involvement" in the kitchen, Fitzgerald continues to model his own kitchen performance after the example set by his mentor.

HOW TO REMOVE THE SKIN FROM A SALMON FILET

★ ★ ★ ★ ★ ★ ★ ★ ★ ★ ★ ★

Throughout my career as a chef, I've learned how to anticipate people's likes and dislikes. Interestingly, a common dislike is salmon skin. This trick for removing fish skin is quick and simple enough for anyone to do at home.

STEP ONE: Heat a pan with a small amount of olive oil until it is smoking hot. Place the fish skin-side down in the pan.

STEP TWO: Sear the fish on one side for 1 minute.

STEP THREE: Peel off the skin. Turn the fish. You can then peel the skin right off with tongs. Season the same side with salt and pepper, and cook the fish for another 2 to 3 minutes or until it is medium rare in the center. Finish with a drizzle of olive oil and freshly squeezed lemon juice.

MORE CHEF'S SECRETS . . .

FM: What do you serve a finicky eater?
DF: Any type of fresh, homemade pasta.

FM: Name an ingredient you can't live without.
DF: I use peppery, Tuscan olive oil in absolutely everything, from salad dressings to pastas. Olive oil is truly a magical ingredient because you can start and finish a dish with it.

FM: What's your favorite restaurant other than your own?
DF: Nobu Next Door in New York City. My wife and I are addicted to the rock shrimp tempura with creamy spicy sauce and love the no-reservations, relaxed environment.

Albert DI MEGLIO

PROFILE

Albert Di Meglio, a graduate of New York Restaurant School, has been working in the industry since he turned fifteen. Although his first job was in a Staten Island pizzeria, Di Meglio went on to become a sous chef under Marc Murphy at Cellar in the Sky and *chef de partie* under Michael Lomonaco at Windows on the World. In 1996, a chance meeting with Le Cirque's executive chef Sottha Khunn landed Di Meglio in the kitchen of that legendary *New York Times* four-star institution, owned by the Maccionis, one of the city's premier restaurant families. Di Meglio is now executive chef of another Maccioni establishment, Osteria del Circo.

HOW TO SEAR A FISH IN A STAINLESS STEEL PAN

★ ★ ★ ★ ★ ★ ★ ★ ★ ★ ★ ★

Despite its smooth appearance, a stainless steel pan is porous, with a lot of tiny holes in the metal from manufacturing. These holes need to be filled with oil before you can properly sear fish in it. Once the holes are filled, your fish will not stick and you will have the crispy skin you've been looking for. For best results, I recommend using a flat stainless steel pan such as an All-Clad sauté pan.

STEP ONE: Place the pan on the fire and let it heat (with no oil or butter in it). This will let the "pores" in the metal open even wider. However, you don't want it to get too hot, or your oil will immediately burn when you put it in.

STEP TWO: While the pan is heating, take the fish you're going to cook (with skin on) and place it on a paper towel to dry.

STEP THREE: Add just enough oil to cover the bottom of the pan. Pour in enough oil to make the pan look shiny, but not so much that the fish will fry. Wait for the oil to slightly smoke, and then lower the flame to medium. Swirl the oil around the pan, waiting about 2 more minutes before you put the fish in.

STEP FOUR: Wipe the pan with the skin side of the fish to determine if the pan is ready. If the fish doesn't stick, place it the pan, skin-side down. If the fish starts sticking, wait a little longer.

STEP FIVE: Press the fish down in the pan. Press it down until the proteins relax and the fish lies flat in the pan. Keep it at a medium heat and continue to cook the fish until the skin begins to crisp up.

STEP SIX: Add a little butter. The butter will add flavor, and it will also help release the fish if it is stuck to the pan. When the butter turns brown, add several sprigs of thyme and one clove of smashed garlic for flavor.

STEP SEVEN: Remove the fish when it just starts to become opaque. Flip it onto the side that wasn't cooked and let it rest before serving.

STEP EIGHT: Wipe down the pan with a dry rag and a little oil. Next time you want fish, cooking with this method will be even easier, because your pan is now cured and ready.

MORE CHEF'S SECRETS . . .

FM: Do you have a culinary hero?
AD: I have many heroes in this industry and beyond. I admire people who work their dreams into reality and do what they love to do.

FM: What's your favorite middle-of-the-night snack?
AD: Definitely peanut butter and jelly.

FM: What's the best cooking advice you've ever gotten?
AD: When Sottha Khunn was the chef at Le Cirque 2000, he told me, "Anybody can cook, but only about 1 percent of would-be chefs make it. You're going to have to bust your rear end to be a chef who makes it."

Ari WEINZWEIG

★ ★ ★ ★ ★ ★ ★

HOW TO TAP INTO THE SECRET LIFE OF ANCHOVIES

★ ★ ★ ★ ★ ★ ★ ★ ★ ★ ★ ★

Although anchovies get a bad rap, I've long believed them to be one of the most amazing and effective ways to add flavor to savory dishes of all sorts. I think anchovies can do for sauces and soups what real vanilla can do for so many baked goods and pastries—provide a depth and complexity of flavor that the eater can't always identify, but that will make for a far more satisfying eating experience. But since so many people think that they don't like them, you usually have to make the addition of the anchovies a covert operation.

STEP ONE: Start with good anchovies. While there are cheap offerings all over the place, they're usually awful. Better anchovies taste better (and usually cost more, too). To my taste, the best are those packed in coarse salt.

STEP TWO: Filet the anchovies. Remove the backbone from the center of the fish (with your fingers); then rinse the anchovy quickly under gently running water to remove any small bones that have been left behind.

STEP THREE: Add a few anchovies to your sauce, soup, or stew in the early stages of cooking. The best time to add them is while you're sautéing vegetables. Within a matter of minutes, the anchovies will melt—you can't see them, but you will definitely enjoy their flavor.

MORE CHEF'S SECRETS . . .

FM: What is the best food journey you ever made?
AW: A trip I took to the mountains of Switzerland, Italy, and France with half a dozen friends to learn about mountain cheeses. Great people, incredible scenery, and amazing cheese is a combination that's hard to beat.

FM: What is the most overrated food find of the last decade?
AW: There are few overrated foods, but lots of mediocre versions of foods that are presented as being really good when they aren't. This is true of bread, cheese, tea, and so forth. There's fancy packaging, a good public relations campaign, but not much flavor.

FM: What is the most undervalued?
AW: The undervalued is always true artisanal food. When you see how much work it is to hand-gather really wild, wild rice, to produce handmade cheese, to bake truly artisanal bread—whatever we all pay, it's a bargain.

Andrew CHASE

PROFILE

Andrew Chase grew up in Nantucket, spending his summers scallop shucking and fishing local waters. Unlike many of his contemporaries, Chase did not attend cooking school. Instead, after acquiring a degree in psychology, he was involved in a restaurant conversion real estate deal. The time he spent in and around kitchens started Chase on a career as a chef. He trained by "cooking around town," working in some of New York's best-loved restaurants, including Union Square Café and Monkey Bar. In 1998, Chase went to France to work as *stagiere* at Emile Jung's Le Crocodile, returning to New York in his first sous chef position at the Mark Hotel under the acclaimed chef Philippe Boulot. In 2001, Chase, known for his frills-free yet sophisticated fare, became the Mark's executive chef.

HOW TO FILET AN EEL

★ ★ ★ ★ ★ ★ ★ ★ ★ ★ ★ ★

I was an American guy working in the famous French restaurant Le Crocodile as *commis* to the *poissonnier*, and part of my day was devoted to cleaning the fish, in particular, the eels—a tedious task that usually took up much of my afternoons, when I should have been at the café like everyone else. The traditional method required me to cut the eel into 3-inch sections and then filet each small piece. When I accompanied Chef Jung on a trip to Japan to do a week of dinners, I was awestruck at how quickly and efficiently the chefs there were able to filet an entire eel. I carried this technique back to France with me, where—not wanting to step on anyone's toes—I cautiously asked the *chef de cuisine* if I could try it. It made me a hero and freed up my afternoons to boot! Here's the trick I learned:

STEP ONE: Impale the eel (with a nail through the head) onto your cutting board (Figure A). Imagining that the eel is a piece of rope, grab the tail end, pull it straight down, and hold it taut.

STEP TWO: Remove the backbone. Using a sharp knife with a stiff, fine-pointed blade, make a long incision right down the spine of the eel (Figure B). The eel will be flayed open like a book, with the backbone exposed. Holding the knife horizontally, slip the blade under the backbone, run it down the length of the eel to release the bone (Figure C), and snap the bone off at the tail end.

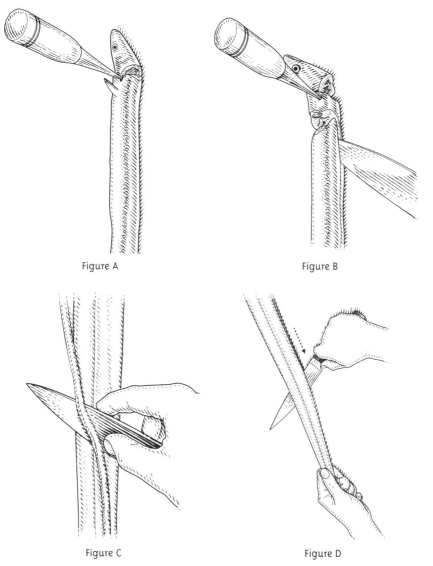

Figure A

Figure B

Figure C

Figure D

STEP THREE: Remove the skin. Continuing to use the knife horizontally (but at a slight angle), cut into the eel, starting at the top, using the blade to lift the meat and separate it from the skin (Figure D). You have now fileted an entire eel in minutes. Proceed to café!

MORE CHEF'S SECRETS . . .

FM: Do you have a kitchen pet peeve?
AC: I'm not a total control freak, but if your cutting board is not perfectly aligned with the edge of your work table, I tend to find it very distracting. Please adjust accordingly.

FM: What's your perfect day off?
AC: I love my city (New York) and like to explore different neighborhoods and cultures. My last day off was great! Tennis in the morning with my wife, and then a drive out to Brighton Beach, which is a Russian neighborhood next to Coney Island. It's got loads of food markets, restaurants, and great people-watching: You really feel like you're in another country. Borscht and blintzes for lunch and then a late-afternoon swim.

FM: What's your favorite piece of art featuring food?
AC: That's a hard question; there's a lot to love. The movie *Tampopo* is a beautiful work representing how food enriches our physical, emotional, and spiritual lives.

HOW TO TENDERIZE OCTOPUS WITH WINE CORKS

★ ★ ★ ★ ★ ★ ★ ★ ★ ★ ★

I read about this technique years ago and have been a devotee ever since. It works because there is an enzyme in cork that helps tenderize the octopus and reduce the cooking time. A general rule of thumb is to use one cork per quart of liquid. The corks can be right out of a wine bottle, no matter if it's red or white or even cleaned. This is how I make a signature dish at Sushi Samba.

STEP ONE: Preheat the oven to 350°F.

STEP TWO: Combine the following in a large saucepan and bring to a simmer:
- ★ 4 quarts water
- ★ 3 1-inch knobs fresh ginger, peeled and sliced
- ★ 1 tablespoon cayenne pepper
- ★ 10 black peppercorns
- ★ 2 bay leaves
- ★ 2 tablespoons ground aji panca (a Peruvian chile with a rich, slightly sweet flavor)
- ★ 1 small bunch parsley stems
- ★ 2 lemons, sliced

STEP THREE: Rub a 2¹/₂-pound fresh octopus with handfuls of coarse salt, as if rubbing moisturizer into skin. When the salt begins to get "frothy," rinse the octopus under cool water and pat it dry. Pound the octopus with a meat tenderizer, or use a clean daikon root for the traditional Japanese method. Rinse and dry again.

Michael CRESSOTTI

★ ★ ★ ★ ★ ★ ★ ★

PROFILE

Young Michael Cressotti accompanied his father, a restaurant supply salesman, on his daily rounds to some of New York City's finest restaurants. After earning a culinary degree from Johnson and Wales University, Cressotti was banquet supervisor at Florida's celebrated Turnberry Isle Resort and Club. While there, he was exposed to a style of food referred to (at the time) as New World Cuisine—a mix of Latin spices and exotic fruits and vegetables combined with French technique and presentation. He took this new skill to New York City as opening sous chef for Douglas Rodriguez at Patria, the Nuevo Latino tour de force and recipient of a three-star review from the *New York Times*. Today, Cressotti serves as "Samba" Chef at New York's Sushi Samba, known for its creative take on Japanese, Brazilian, and Peruvian cuisines.

STEP FOUR: Add 3 wine corks to the liquid and slowly lower the octopus in.
When the tentacles begin to curl, remove the pan from the heat and place it in the oven until the octopus is tender, 1 to 1½ hours.

STEP FIVE: Serve. At Sushi Samba, we serve this dish "salad style." The sliced octopus is tossed with *mâche* (a green also called "lamb's lettuce" or "corn salad"), peppers, scallions, and a smoked paprika vinaigrette, and served on a plate that has been dusted with smoked paprika and garnished with a grilled half lime (dipped in sugar to caramelize).

MORE CHEF'S SECRETS . . .

FM: Best thing about Brazilian food?
MC: Lots of flavor; simple, old-style cooking technique; one-pot meals.

FM: You're about to have your last meal. What is it?
MC: Fried oysters from Blue Ribbon in New York City.

FM: Best kitchen habit anyone can develop?
MC: Cleanliness and organization. The benefits are self-evident.

HOW TO TURN OUT TENDER SHRIMP

★ ★ ★ ★ ★ ★ ★ ★ ★ ★ ★ ★

You might not know this, but 30 minutes of brining ensures tender, succulent shrimp every time, regardless of the cooking method. I discovered this technique on my own after successfully brining other types of meat—mostly pork, chicken, and turkey. After experimenting with shrimp one day, I was blown away by how sweet and tender they were. Brining may take a little extra time, but it's absolutely worth it.

STEP ONE: Make the brining solution. For each pound of shrimp, combine 2 quarts water, $1/4$ cup salt, and $1/4$ cup sugar in a large mixing bowl. Whisk together until the salt and sugar dissolve.

Mark FILIPPO

★ ★ ★ ★ ★ ★ ★ ★

PROFILE

Mark Filippo attended New York City Technical College's hotel/restaurant management school and did a summer apprenticeship at the Georges V in Paris. After working his way through such New York institutions as Le Chantilly, Quilted Giraffe, New York Metro (with friend and classmate Patrick Clark), and Adrienne at the Peninsula Hotel, Filippo settled at Cafe Mezé in Hartsdale, New York. Here he turns out Mediterranean cuisine that is flavorful and sophisticated, the result of his cutting-edge creativity and use of fine, fresh ingredients.

STEP TWO: Soak the shrimp. Place the peeled and deveined shrimp in the brine solution, and allow them to sit untouched for 30 minutes at room temperature.

STEP THREE: Drain, dry, and cook. Drain the shrimp in a colander and gently pat them dry with paper towels. Proceed with your favorite recipe: pan-fry, grill, or sauté. The shrimp always turn out moist and delicious.

MORE CHEF'S SECRETS . . .

FM: What's the best time of the year to cook?
MF: Summer, because I get amazing local produce, fish, and meat. I love creating light, flavorful dishes without a lot of fat, and having incredibly fresh ingredients makes that process simple and enjoyable.

FM: What's your favorite kitchen snack?
MF: Although it's bad for my waistline, bread.

FM: Which aisle do you go down first at the grocery store?
MF: I always go down the produce aisle first because I design my menu around the fruits and vegetables I select.

HOW TO SPRINKLE IN SHRIMP FLAVOR

★ ★ ★ ★ ★ ★ ★ ★ ★ ★ ★ ★ ★

The first time I saw dried shrimp was when I was working for chef and Asian food expert Bruce Cost at Monsoon in San Francisco, and I remember thinking, "What the hell is this?" The shrimp, which are shelled, salted, and dried, are usually sold in plastic bags in different quantities and sizes. As I experimented with different ways to use the dried shrimp, I found that grinding them essentially turned an ingredient into a seasoning. Here's how to get shrimp flakes so light that they melt upon contact with liquid.

STEP ONE: Place the dried shrimp in the bowl of a food processor fitted with a metal blade; pulse until they are broken up into smaller pieces.

STEP TWO: Transfer small batches of the shrimp pieces to a spice or coffee grinder used exclusively for grinding spices and process for several minutes until finely ground. The shrimp will fluff up like cotton candy or insulation.

STEP THREE: Store the shrimp flakes in an airtight container. The shrimp won't spoil, but if you don't seal the container, everything else in their vicinity will soon smell like fish food.

STEP FOUR: Sprinkle the shrimp into a risotto, into a stock, or over linguine—any place you want to add the flavor of shrimp. However, be

Joe JACK

★ ★ ★ ★ ★ ★ ★ ★

PROFILE

Native Iowan Joe Jack, who began cooking while in high school, embarked upon his professional culinary career in San Francisco in such landmark places as Monsoon under Bruce Cost and Tony Gulisano, and again with Gulisano at Chow. Jack was also chef at Tutto Bene, Tutto Mare, and Sunny Jim's and spent a year cooking in the Umbria region of Italy before opening Luna Park in San Francisco and Los Angeles, and San Francisco's Mission District's Last Supper Club with business partner and manager A. J. Gilbert.

aware of allergies: Just because you can't see the shrimp doesn't mean they aren't there, and people who are allergic to shellfish will have the same reaction to eating food that has been seasoned with dried shrimp flakes as if they'd eaten a whole, fresh shrimp.

MORE CHEF'S SECRETS . . .

FM: Silliest eighties food trend?
JJ: Squeeze-bottle stuff. It ruined restaurant food for such a long time because people thought that without it, food wasn't fancy. We lost "simple."

FM: Favorite hometown food?
JJ: Rudy's Tacos in Davenport, Iowa.

FM: Best food store?
JJ: Any *alimentari* in Italy.

HOW TO ACHIEVE SAND-FREE CLAMS

Paul WADE

★ ★ ★ ★ ★ ★ ★ ★ ★ ★ ★ ★ ★

In my restaurant, finding sandy, grainy clams in any dish is intolerable. But even with all the "boutique growing" principles being applied to food, nothing can be done about the sand. Unlike mussels, which are rope cultivated these days (and sand free), clams still need to be under sand and soil to grow. My method for using electricity and fresh water to remove the sand was taught to me years ago—by whom, I don't remember, and how they discovered it, I don't know. But I can tell you this—food preparation legends and myths exist far and wide in professional kitchens. In my first few years of training, I was astounded by the insights and lore that abound.

STEP ONE: Wash the clams under running water. Use a brush to scrub away the last vestiges of mud and sand until the water runs clear. Do not use a colander until you are draining and drying the clams after washing.

STEP TWO: Create an electrical charge with a stainless steel spoon and water. Put the clams in the sink, and then fill it with cold water. Let the water run from the faucet down the back of a stainless steel spoon and into the basin. (The electrical charge is created by water flowing over the stainless steel; electrostatic discharge/charged particles is the physics behind it all.) The clams will spit out the sand as well as the fluid in their systems as a reaction to the fresh water and electricity. It is important to keep them submerged in fresh water so they process it through their bivalves. It's known as "spitting." The whole process is about 10 minutes to sandless clams.

MORE CHEF'S SECRETS . . .

FM: If you wrote a screenplay about the restaurant business, what would you call it?
PW: *Prix Fixe: Instructions for Life.*

FM: What's a terrible kitchen habit that you will not tolerate?
PW: Lack of integrity, passion, or cleanliness.

FM: What's the best kitchen habit anyone can develop?
PW: Patience, cleanliness, drive, and discipline.

PAUL WADE'S SHELLFISH BOUILLABAISSE

FOR CROSTINI:

1 baguette

6 tablespoons garlic butter

$^1/_4$ cup chopped parsley

FOR BOUILLABAISSE:

1 pound black mussels, fresh in
   the shell

1 pound green mussels, fresh in
   the shell

1$^1/_2$ pounds clams, fresh in the shell

1 cup butter, divided

2 tablespoons chopped shallots

2 tablespoons chopped garlic

1 quart white wine

1 quart clam juice

24 diver scallops, dry pack,
   feet removed

16 large shrimp, peeled and
   deveined

$^1/_2$ cup chopped parsley

Salt and pepper to taste

Cut the baguette on a bias into 16 pieces. Coat one side of each piece with garlic butter and toast until lightly browned. Sprinkle with $^1/_4$ cup parsley and set aside.

Put the washed mussels and clams in a large pot with a bit of the butter, and heat until they start to open. Add the shallots and garlic, then the wine and clam juice. Then add the scallops, shrimp, and remaining butter. Cover and steam for 3 minutes. Do not boil. Remove from heat and allow to stand for a few minutes so the shellfish finish cooking.

Place two crostini in the bottom of each of eight large bowls. Arrange the seafood on top of the crostini, then pour the pan sauce over the top, dividing it evenly among the bowls. Garnish with remaining parsley, season with salt and pepper, and serve.

Makes 8 servings

Cory SCHREIBER

★ ★ ★ ★ ★

HOW TO FIRE-ROAST OYSTERS

★ ★ ★ ★ ★ ★ ★ ★ ★ ★ ★ ★

If you roast oysters over an open flame—on the beach or a wood fire—the accepted custom is to wait until the shells pop open before removing them from the heat. But if you wait for that indicator, the oysters will actually be overcooked. Instead, look for the steam. Here's how.

STEP ONE: Before cooking, oysters should be reintroduced into their natural environment (or as close as one can get to it). Once purchased from the store, soak oysters in salted water that is changed twice a day, using 1 quart water to 2 tablespoons salt. This will ensure that the oysters stay plump and tasty, retaining some saltwater flavor. If the oyster shells are dirty, they can be washed and scrubbed. But in my opinion, you don't eat the shell, so why bother?

STEP TWO: Suspend the oysters on a wire grate or rack over a well-built fire.

STEP THREE: When steam is released from the shell seams, pull the oyster off the direct fire and let it stand over a slightly cooler area. The true telltale sign of doneness is a light vapor of steam that will be released from the shell seams. At this point, pull the oysters off the center coals of the fire and drag them to a lower-temperature area on the edges of the rack. If the fire does not allow for a cooler spot, remove them to a plate or cooling rack away from the fire.

STEP FOUR: Shuck the oyster with ease, as the shell pops right open. There is a dilemma in my long family line of oyster fanaticism about which end to put the knife in when you open an oyster. I open mine from the rear or hinge area because it allows a firm planting of the knife (between the shells) and some leverage (from which to push up to separate the shells) before peeling away the oyster from the connective muscle. This technique is used by the mass factory shuckers, so they get a more beautiful oyster for packing.

But here is a method my cousin Chris from Oysterville swears by. He goes though the front (or thin plate area) of the oyster and separates the shell (without the leverage from the hinge). This method is used for speed, but does not offer cosmetic beauty, as the thin part of the shell will crack easily and the knife can puncture the flesh of the oyster.

STEP FIVE: Add a squeeze of lemon juice, a drizzle of olive oil, some fresh-ground black pepper, and serve.

MORE CHEF'S SECRETS . . .

FM: It's your birthday. What's for dinner?
CS: My birthday is in April. So, for dinner that night is steamed fresh Dungeness crab with boiled new potatoes and crunchy crisp coleslaw, and then good Oregon cheese and dried fruit for dessert. Oregon Sauvignon Blanc with the crab, and 4- to 5-year-old Oregon Pinot Noir with the cheese.

FM: Favorite food movie?
CS: *Big Night*, or the old *Who Is Killing the Great Chefs of Europe?*

FM: Kitchen nightmare?
CS: Ansul system [fire suppression system] going off in the middle of service. No turning back, no food survives, and everything gets thrown out. It's time to start over, as they say.

Bradford THOMPSON

HOW TO TENDERIZE A LOBSTER

★ ★ ★ ★ ★ ★ ★ ★ ★ ★ ★ ★

When my family went on vacations to Maine, we cooked lobsters in the standard way—in a big pot of boiling water until they were bright red, which we thought meant that they were done (but over-done was more like it). They always seemed so rubbery! While I was the banquet chef at Daniel, I cooked an average of 200 lobsters per week, so after thousands of lobsters over the years, I found that the best way to get a tender piece of lobster is a slow, gentle cooking technique. Instead of boiling the lobster and then shocking it in ice water, I pour boiling liquid over the lobsters and let them sit in it until they cook. This technique yields a very tender piece of meat because the lobster isn't cooking in a violent atmosphere or undergoing radical changes in temperature.

STEP ONE: Choose the right lobsters. Go to a reputable fishmonger or market and buy live lobsters from a tank. When selecting lobster, you want the liveliest and strongest of the lot. For home cooking, $1^{1}/_{4}$- to $1^{1}/_{2}$-pounders are the best size—they are easiest to deal with and will stay tender when cooked with the right technique. Note that winter lobster, known as hardshell, tends to be meatier, because the meat-to-shell ratio is higher.

STEP TWO: Place the lobsters in a bucket or stockpot large enough for the lobsters to be totally submerged in liquid.

STEP THREE: Pour simmering Court Bouillon (see recipe on page 96) over the lobsters. Let them sit for 3 minutes if your recipe calls for reheating or 8 minutes if they are being served cold.

STEP FOUR: Twist off the tails, and resubmerge the body and claws in the liquid to continue cooking. Since the claws take longer to cook than the tails, use clean dishwashing gloves to reach in and twist the tails off, returning the body and claws to the liquid for an additional 1 to 2 minutes.

MORE CHEF'S SECRETS . . .

FM: Favorite holiday meal?
BT: Thanksgiving, even though I always work. I still cook for my staff or friends after work. It's a great holiday because it's all about eating and sharing with friends and family (and football). It also incorporates so many traditions for so many people, and it usually involves a specific dish of a region or culture or the season. It is also one of the few times that American families and friends actually sit and eat at the same time and at the same table.

FM: Most prized kitchen possession?
BT: One of the things that gets the most use in our kitchen is our Vitamix blender—it is simply the best. For me personally, my knives are the thing that I use every day and are like an extension of my hand. But one of my most prized possessions is a simple instrument that I bought in Umbria—my *chittara* to make handcut spaghetti. It took me years to find.

FM: Ingredient you can't live without?
BT: You can't cook without onions and garlic, which I use in almost everything I make. But if I had to pick one thing—pork.

COURT BOUILLON

This is a flavored poaching liquid typically used for fish and shellfish.

2 gallons water
2 cups white wine
1 teaspoon whole black peppercorns
1 teaspoon fennel seeds
1 teaspoon coriander seeds
1 bay leaf
2 sprigs fresh thyme
Pinch dried red chili flakes
1 orange, halved
1 lemon, halved
1 leek, split and washed
1 onion, quartered
1 carrot, cut into large dice
2 celery stalks, cut into large dice
3 garlic cloves, peeled and smashed
$^1/_4$ cup coarse salt

Combine all the ingredients in a large stockpot; bring to a boil and reduce to a simmer for about 20 minutes so that it carries the flavors when the fish or shellfish is added.

HOW TO SHELL A COOKED LOBSTER

★ ★ ★ ★ ★ ★ ★ ★ ★ ★ ★ ★

Picking, or removing, the meat from a lobster is similar to the process for eating a whole lobster at the table. The difference is that you'll be wearing an apron instead of a plastic bib. You'll also have serious kitchen utensils at your disposal, and the lobster won't be hot, so it will be easier to handle. We learned this technique for shelling cooked lobster while working for Jeremiah Tower at Stars in San Francisco. He had grown up on the East Coast and had spent time in Maine, so he knew a lot about lobster and used it frequently on his menu. Over the years we've lived in Maine, we've perfected our own technique.

STEP ONE: First, the tail.

★ Holding the lobster right side up, twist the tail off the body (Figure A).

★ Hold the separated tail right side up, and break off the tail fins by bending them upward. This will reveal a hole in the tail cavity.

★ Insert the tine of a fork or your fingers into the hole and gently dislodge the meat by pushing it out through the other end of the tail (Figure B).

★ Using a chef's knife, make a small lengthwise incision along the back (actually the top side) of the tail meat, just deep enough to reveal the dark, thin intestine (Figure C). Remove and discard.

★ Cut the tail into several large medallions, or leave whole, as the recipe dictates.

Mark GAIER & Clark FRASIER

★ ★ ★ ★ ★ ★ ★ ★ ★

PROFILE

Ohio native Mark Gaier and Californian Clark Frasier, who worked with some of the country's finest chefs, including Jeremiah Tower, formed a business partnership that acquired Arrows Restaurant in Ogunquit, Maine. Utilizing their extensive travel and training, they have created a classic country restaurant that has continually garnered national and international accolades for its outstanding cuisine, flawless service, beautiful setting, and award-winning wine list. In 1992, the chefs began, out of necessity, to develop a kitchen garden that today has grown to almost two acres in size and provides the restaurant with 80 percent of the menu each evening in season. Arrows was named one of the Top 50 Restaurants in the country by *Gourmet*. Gaier and Frasier are also the authors of *The Arrows Cookbook*.

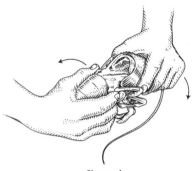

Figure A

Figure B

Figure C

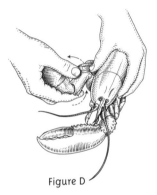

Figure D

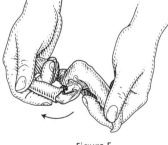

Figure E

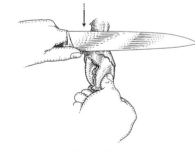

Figure F

STEP TWO: Next, the claws.

★ With a firm grip, twist the claws off at the knuckles. Then twist the claws off where they meet the body (Figure D).

★ Grasp the small pincer of each claw and bend it backward until it breaks off (Figure E). The meat inside the pincer might stay attached to the claw meat, but if not, remove the meat from the broken piece of shell by tapping the shell on the counter and shaking it out, or insert a toothpick and pull the meat out.

★ Using the back of a cleaver or chef's knife (Figure F), crack the claws just deeply enough so the shells can be pried open and the meat removed (too deep, and you'll smash the meat). Or, cut the claw open with sturdy kitchen shears. Remove the translucent cartilage running through the middle of the claw, and cut the meat.

STEP THREE: Now, the knuckles and legs.

★ Use the back of a cleaver or chef's knife to crack open the knuckles. (You can also use kitchen shears.) Pull the meat from the knuckles.

★ If you don't want to waste any lobster, you can remove tiny bits of meat from the walking claws, commonly referred to as the legs. Pull them off the body, break them in half at the joint, and line them up on a cutting board. Run a rolling pin perpendicularly over the claws and the meat will pop out. Many people don't bother with this step and instead add the walking claws (and the rest of the lobster carcass) to vegetable or chicken stock.

MORE CHEF'S SECRETS . . .

FM: Kitchen motto?
MG & CF: Always salt.

FM: Best food city other than your own?
MG & CF: Chicago.

FM: Favorite bar snack?
MG & CF: Roasted peanuts with chiles.

CHAPTER FOUR

★ ★ ★ ★

PRODUCE

Eric TORRALBA

★　★　★　★　★

PROFILE

Executive chef Eric Torralba brings more than twenty years of experience in world-class establishments to the restaurant at the California vineyard of Domaine Chandon. The French-born chef's passion for the culinary arts began at an early age in the open-air marketplace in Cannes. After attending the culinary academy L'Ecole d'Hôtellerie in Nice, Torralba worked in the kitchens of Jean Louis Palladin, Roger Vergé, and Paul Bocuse. He also spent seven years as executive chef aboard *Savarona*, the world's largest privately owned yacht, before extending his global experience to the Napa Valley, a place that he says feels like "home in the South of France."

HOW TO KEEP COOKED GREEN VEGETABLES CRISP AND COLORFUL

★　★　★　★　★　★　★　★　★　★　★

When blanching green vegetables, all you have to do in order to retain the chlorophyll, and therefore the color and the nutritional value, is immerse them in cold water until they are thoroughly chilled. It seems too easy, but it works.

STEP ONE: Put the vegetables in a bowl of cold water. Fill a mixing bowl with several trays of ice cubes and cold water, or fill a bowl with cold water and place it in the freezer for about 30 minutes. Add the vegetables, and leave them in the water until they are thoroughly chilled.

STEP TWO: Boil water, and add the vegetables. Bring a large pot of abundantly salted water (gray sea salt is best) to a boil. Using a slotted spoon to leave as much cold water as possible in the bowl, transfer the vegetables to the boiling water. Return the bowl to the freezer to keep the water as cold as possible. Cook the vegetables until they are just short of the desired doneness—the timing will vary from vegetable to vegetable, but you should always aim for a crisp-tender texture.

STEP THREE: Return the cooked vegetables to the cold water. Use a slotted spoon to retrieve the vegetables (draining excess water) and plunge them back into the ice water in order to stop the cooking process. This can be done several hours before you plan to serve the vegetables—before serving, just reheat them in a pan with a small amount of melted butter and olive oil.

MORE CHEF'S SECRETS . . .

FM: Can you describe your cooking style?
ET: I have come to believe in the "sixth sense" in food: *Ce sont les sens qui donnent un sens à la vie—l'emotion et la magie* (It's the senses that give sense [meaning] to life—emotion and magic).

FM: What is your most dreaded kitchen chore?
ET: Cooking for people who do not share my passion for food.

FM: What's the best thing about being a chef?
ET: Exploring all aspects of creativity and being paid for it.

Douglas KATZ

PROFILE

Douglas Katz, who grew up in Shaker Heights, Ohio, started cooking when he was seven. A self-proclaimed "fat kid who could not stay away from the kitchen," Katz received a bachelor's degree in hotel and restaurant management from the University of Denver and is a graduate of the Culinary Institute of America. After working at the Boston Harbor Hotel, the Little Nell Hotel in Aspen, Colorado, the Wildwood Restaurant in Portland, Oregon, and Moxie in Beechwood, Ohio, he returned to Shaker Heights and opened Fire, named one of the Best New Restaurants by *Esquire* as well as one of America's Best Restaurants by *Gourmet*.

HOW TO CRISP TENDER GREENS

★ ★ ★ ★ ★ ★ ★ ★ ★ ★ ★ ★

When I worked at the Little Nell Hotel in Aspen, Colorado, executive chef George Mahaffey taught me this technique: Use warm water to refresh greens and then chill them in order to get them crisp. As with flowers, if the old stem of the greens is cut or torn to allow the water to be absorbed into the freshly cut end, the greens get crisper.

STEP ONE: Fill your sink with warm water.
The temperature should be 105° to 110°F—if it feels warm to your wrist, it is warm enough.

STEP TWO: Submerge lettuces, herbs, or other tender greens and soak for 5 to 10 minutes.

STEP THREE: Carefully dry the greens, preferably using a salad spinner. Gently shake the greens to remove excess water before spinning. Don't overload the spinner or spin them too quickly, as the greens may bruise.

STEP FOUR: Cover and chill. Cover the greens with a damp towel, chill for at least 30 minutes, and you will once again have crisp, vibrant lettuces, herbs, or greens.

MORE CHEF'S SECRETS . . .

FM: Single best culinary discovery?
DK: Seasoning properly—it heightens the flavor and depth of all food. If you know how to use salt and pepper correctly, you don't need much else.

FM: Who's a cooking legend?
DK: Jack Tripper from *Three's Company*. He was the first passionate cook I remember watching on television.

FM: First thing you do when you get to work?
DK: Say hello to each employee personally.

Ken VEDRINSKI

HOW TO USE BEETS TO MAKE A BEURRE ROUGE (RED BUTTER SAUCE)

★ ★ ★ ★ ★ ★ ★ ★ ★ ★ ★ ★ ★

The problem with beurre rouge (or red butter sauce) is that once red wine is reduced, the color turns brownish. Also, as you cook the wine down, the tannins become more pronounced. I learned this trick for keeping the sauce red by watching Carrie Nahabedian, saucier at Four Seasons, Chicago. Using beets is a totally natural way to give the sauce sweetness. It also keeps the brilliant color of a good red wine.

STEP ONE: Peel and thinly slice one beet. I prefer to use a beet with a 3-inch diameter, because smaller beets are easier to handle. As you slice the beet, bear in mind that the more surface exposed, the more color will bleed, which, in this case, is what you want.

STEP TWO: Prepare the sauce. Melt 1 tablespoon of unsalted butter in a heavy saucepan. Add 2 shallots (peeled and sliced), half a fresh bay leaf, 1 garlic clove (slivered), and several crushed peppercorns, and cook, stirring occasionally, until the shallots are soft, about 3 minutes. Now add the beets and stir until they begin to give up their color, another 3 minutes or so. Add 1 bottle of good red wine and reduce to a quarter.

STEP THREE: Strain the sauce through a fine-mesh sieve.

STEP FOUR: Slowly whisk in $1/2$ cup of slightly softened unsalted butter, bit by bit. Season to taste with salt.

MORE CHEF'S SECRETS . . .

FM: First thing you do when you get to work?
KV: Sit down and go through everything that came in and then write a daily menu.

FM: Food hero?
KV: Like many other chefs, I'd say Thomas Keller of the French Laundry. His food is so intelligent. He has a way of making food exciting but accessible. His preparations show great thought and care.

FM: An ingredient you can't live without?
KV: Fresh fish.

Joël
ANTUNES

* * * * * * * * *

PROFILE

Joël Antunes's commitment to French cuisine began in his grandmother's kitchen in the south of France. Antunes officially began his culinary training in 1975 and has been chef at such prestigious restaurants as Ledoyen and Duquesnoy in Paris and the Hotel Negresco in Nice. He worked under celebrated French pastry chef Yves Thuriès and served as *chef poissonnier* for the legendary Paul Bocuse in Lyons before settling in the United States and opening his own restaurant, Joël, in Atlanta, named one of America's Best New Restaurants by *Gourmet* and *Esquire*.

HOW TO IMPROVE THE CONSISTENCY OF A TOMATO

★ ★ ★ ★ ★ ★ ★ ★ ★ ★ ★ ★

I have always prided myself on making fresh ice creams and sorbets, both savory and sweet. In the early production days, however, I noticed that I was not getting a consistently frozen savory tomato sorbet; sometimes it would be more like a snow cone with liquid at the bottom than a well-integrated sorbet. One time I happened to notice that my line cook had put the tomatoes for the next round of sorbet production in the freezer, and that her sorbet turned out perfectly! From that moment on, I practiced the same method of freezing tomatoes (prior to peeling) for any sorbet or sauce production.

STEP ONE: Lay out the tomatoes on parchment paper on any flat surface—a ceramic casserole dish, cookie sheet, or metal baking rack.

STEP TWO: Freeze at about 30°F for 20 minutes. Freezing a tomato changes its molecular structure—ice crystals form from the outside in, and ice takes up more space than water. The liquid inside the frozen tomatoes has crystallized and somewhat expanded, so that after defrosting, the crystals have already expanded and the tomatoes are more readily liquefiable. An analogy: A peach that has been frozen will more readily break apart when it's defrosted, because the ice crystals (expanded water) have broken the natural fibrous structure of the peach. The same thing applies with tomatoes.

STEP THREE: Use your previously frozen tomatoes in any of the following:
- ★ **Spaghetti sauce:** Remember to add a pinch of sugar and Worcestershire sauce to balance the tomatoes' acidity.
- ★ **Savory tomato sorbet:** Classy gourmet garnish for gazpacho.
- ★ **Pizza:** Fresh tomatoes add juiciness to prevent dry pizza.
- ★ **Ratatouille:** Slightly pulpy and lightly pulsed tomatoes add flowing texture to your other sautéed vegetables.

MORE CHEF'S SECRETS . . .

FM: Favorite food city other than your own?
JA: London.

FM: Ingredient you can't live without?
JA: *Fleur de sel* (salt flowers), which looks like micro basil with salt crystals in the center.

FM: Best bar snack ever?
JA: Anchovies sautéed with red pepper sauce.

JOËL ANTUNES'S TIPS ON CHOOSING A GOOD TOMATO

★ First of all—**smell**. Ninety percent of the action of tasting is actually input from your nose, not your mouth. So smell the tomatoes first. Do they smell like good earth? Do they smell slightly sweet? These are good signs.

★ Then **read the sales charts posted with each variety of tomato**. Have they ever been refrigerated? To preserve the fresh appearance of tomatoes, growers send tomatoes to market in refrigerated trucks; sometimes it's best to visit the local farms and farmers' markets for a fresher, never-been-refrigerated product.

★ Last in importance when choosing tomatoes is their **appearance and size**. Sometimes "uglier" or asymmetrical tomatoes will indicate a more home-grown organic product, whereas the perfectly round, extra-large tomatoes can be a product of a more "manufactured" growing environment. A tomato's size is important: Traditionally, artisanally grown tomatoes will not exceed current standards of small to medium size, and again this is an important indication of farmer-grown versus "manufactured" tomatoes.

★ Bottom line, though, is **pick something that smells like sweet, warm earth and appeals to you aesthetically.** Good produce markets might even let you have a taste, too!

HOW TO PEEL A TOMATO WITH A BLOWTORCH

★ ★ ★ ★ ★ ★ ★ ★ ★ ★ ★ ★

Taking a step back to analyze the task at hand often reveals that it makes sense to revise some age-old methods. When I thought about how we fire-roast peppers—blistering the skin to peel them—it only made sense to peel the skin of a tomato the same way, instead of dipping it in boiling water. Any culinary blowtorch (available in most kitchen stores) will work. By using this technique, not only are you avoiding unnecessary steps while keeping a much cleaner work area, you are avoiding cooking the tomato and are keeping it from becoming waterlogged. You end up with a product in as close to its natural state as you can get, except that it has been peeled. Here's how to do it.

STEP ONE: Place a whole tomato stem-side down on a metal sheet pan. If you are peeling several tomatoes at once, place them roughly 2 to 3 inches apart on the sheet pan to allow yourself room to move the blowtorch between them.

STEP TWO: Blister the skin of the tomato with the blowtorch. Move the torch in a circular motion roughly 2 to 3 inches away from the to-mato (Figure A). Blister from top to bottom, going all the way around and down to where the tomato rests on the tray. Then carefully turn it over to expose the stem end and blister the top third. You will now have a completely blistered tomato.

J. Bryce WHITTLESEY

★ ★ ★ ★ ★ ★ ★ ★ ★ ★ ★

PROFILE

J. Bryce Whittlesey, educated at the Culinary Institute of America, worked at Boston's L'Espalier and at the Chanticleer in Nantucket before undertaking a career move to France. After his first job at the Hotel Meurice, he continued a five-year tenure that included Michel Rostang in Paris, L'Ousteau de la Baumanière in Provence, and the Hotel Negresco in Nice. Returning to the United States, he worked as *chef de cuisine* at Keswick Hall in Charlottesville, Virginia, and was the executive sous chef for the opening year of the newly renovated Williamsburg Inn. Most recently, Whittlesey's refined style of French-American cooking landed him the executive chef position at the world-class Wheatleigh Hotel in Lenox, Massachusetts.

STEP THREE: Remove the skin. Allow the tomato to cool a few minutes. Using the tip of a paring knife, peel the skin by pulling it away and off the tomato (Figure B).

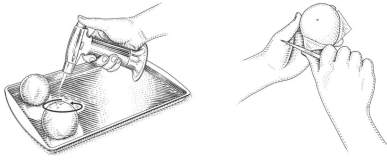

Figure A   Figure B

MORE CHEF'S SECRETS . . .

FM: What qualities make a great regular customer?
JBW: Consistently on time for his/her reservation; knows the staff by name as well as their responsibilities and functions; well-versed in various cuisines so that he/she understands our creativity and style; open to new, more daring dishes.

FM: Any advice for the home cook?
JBW: Keep it simple! Invest in the finest and freshest products available and prepare them in a simple way so as to not mask their flavors.

FM: Favorite music to listen to when you cook?
JBW: I was exposed to the music of world-class singer Charles Aznavour when I took the train to work every morning in Paris. There were always musicians on the trains, and they always seemed to be playing his songs.

HOW TO PEEL TINY PEAR TOMATOES

★ ★ ★ ★ ★ ★ ★ ★ ★ ★ ★ ★ ★

Pear tomatoes are great to serve in the winter because they grow everywhere—Mexico, California, Chile—and so the quality is good all year. Pear tomatoes are also great because you can put the whole thing in your mouth at once and bite. They will explode in your mouth, filling it with tomato flavor. With pear tomatoes, you want to look for a thin skin and sweetness with a touch of acidity. They should be deep red and plump. (If they are hard, they are no good. If they are too soft, they are no good. If they are old, they will have wrinkles like an old man's face.) Although these tiny, sweet, and tender tomatoes are often eaten raw, when you want to use them in a warm dish, like risotto, they should be slipped out of their skins.

STEP ONE: Wash the tomatoes in cool water and dry thoroughly. Lay the tomatoes on a couple of paper towels and roll them around to dry. Poke each tomato with a paring knife to break the skin.

STEP TWO: In a deep pot or deep fryer, heat enough vegetable oil to cover the tomatoes in a single layer and then several inches above that level. Heat the oil until it is almost smoking—you will know it's hot enough when a few water droplets flicked from your fingertips spatter immediately upon contact with the oil.

STEP THREE: *Carefully* put the tomatoes in oil.

Chris QUINTILE

PROFILE

Since beginning his culinary career at age sixteen, Chris Quintile has had a passion for Northern Italian cooking, fostered in the kitchen of his Tuscan grandfather. Quintile attended Parsons School of Design and the Culinary Institute of America before settling in at Chicago's one sixtyblue, working under executive chef Martial Noguier and executive chef Patrick Robertson. He then joined Ristorante We as a sous chef, where he was part of the team that earned the restaurant a three-star review in both the *Chicago Tribune* and *Chicago* magazine. Elevated to *chef de cuisine*, Quintile led the restaurant as it maintained its three-star status and was named one of Chicago's Finest Restaurants by *Chicago* magazine.

Use a strainer to lower them into the oil, but make sure it has a long handle because the oil will splatter. The tomatoes will sink in the oil and seem like they are not doing anything, but in 2 to 10 seconds all hell will break loose. The skins will begin to break in the heat and the moisture released into the oil will create a small storm in your kitchen.

STEP FOUR: As soon as the oil begins to boil, remove your tomatoes and drop them into ice water. The water should have enough ice to cool the tomatoes immediately.

STEP FIVE: When the tomatoes are cold, simply slip the skins off and discard. Place the peeled tomatoes on a tray so you do not crush your delicate little morsels. Use them in any dish where you want their sweet flavor and tender pulp without their tough little skins.

MORE CHEF'S SECRETS . . .

FM: Romantic notion about the restaurant business you would like to dispel?
CQ: There really isn't much romance to being a chef or working in the restaurant business. It is plain, back-breaking hard work to create good food in a busy restaurant.

FM: Uphold?
CQ: The romantic notion that restaurants and kitchens are a great place to interact with people. Working in a kitchen and sweatin' all night and pushing yourself to put out quality food as fast as possible creates so many different situations that it is a great place for people to really get to know one another and create relationships.

FM: Advice for people on their first day in your kitchen?
CQ: Keep your head down and focus. Taste everything! Trust your instincts. You've been eating your whole life; you already know what tastes right and wrong. Ask questions and attack everything. You are better off making a mistake attacking than being timid.

HOW TO DRY TOMATOES IN A CONVECTION OVEN

★ ★ ★ ★ ★ ★ ★ ★ ★ ★ ★ ★

Dick ERATH

We grow so many tomatoes in our garden patch that there is no way we can eat them all while they are fresh. I tried drying them outside, but we are not in Southern Italy; it was hot enough during the day, but the dampness at night molded the tomatoes. I decided to see what I could do in my convection oven. I knew I needed to prop the door open so the moisture could escape and the tomatoes would dry out. The first time, I used a wooden spoon, but it was too heavy and fell out. Then I decided to try a cork (God knows there are plenty of them around here), and it was perfect: lightweight with a good grip. If you like sundried tomatoes, then you'll love making your own. No sun and no farm needed!

STEP ONE: Arrange the tomatoes on a cookie sheet. Halve several ripe Roma tomatoes lengthwise and scoop out the seeds with the side and tip of your thumb. Place the tomatoes, cut-side up, on a cookie sheet, and lightly salt them.

STEP TWO: Place the tomatoes in the oven. Position the pan in the center of the oven. If you are using more than one cookie sheet, make sure the racks are well separated; place them so that they divide the oven into thirds.

STEP THREE: Prop open the oven door with a wine cork. Place the cork lengthwise between the top of the door and the oven.

STEP FOUR: Adjust the oven temperature. Heat the oven on its lowest setting. Hold the probe of an instant-read oven thermometer (the kind with the probe on a long cord) in the gap made by the cork so that the warm air coming out will register on the dial. Adjust the oven setting until the air is registering 130° to 135°F. Maintaining that temperature, the drying time is 8 to 10 hours (depending on the thickness of the tomatoes). When they're ready, the skins will be shriveled or puckered and the underside will look dry.

STEP FIVE: Prepare the dried tomatoes for storage. Coat the tomatoes with a small amount of balsamic vinegar until they are dampened, not swimming. Pack them in a jar and cover the tomatoes with high-quality olive oil. Voilà! The tomatoes can be stored in the sealed jar for several weeks.

MORE CHEF'S SECRETS . . .

FM: Do you have a favorite moment in the process of making wine?
DE: I always look forward to the first press-load of pinot, when the raw wine is draining away from the skins and seeds and you can smell how good the wine is going to be.

FM: Is there something that gives you a sense that the grapes are going to have a particularly good year?
DE: I can tell when we taste the grapes, which I like to do by sticking my head into the vines and biting off clusters without even touching them with my hands.

FM: Do you have a vintner hero?
DE: The late Andre Tchelistcheff, an internationally respected vintner and leader in the California wine industry for more than half a century, who often stopped here for lunch on his way to a consulting job in Washington State. He was particularly inspirational because of his feeling for the whole aspect of wine growing.

HOW TO PEEL AND PIT AN AVOCADO

★ ★ ★ ★ ★ ★ ★ ★ ★ ★ ★ ★

I've been preparing avocados ever since I was a kid. I grew up in Mexico, where avocados are plentiful and used just about every day. Almost every Mexican household keeps avocados on the kitchen table, easily accessible as a condiment to complement other dishes. In my family we'd just reach for an avocado during a meal and cut a slice to put on our rice. At Rosa Mexicano, we go through cases of avocados every week, mostly to make our signature guacamole. To find a perfectly ripe avocado, gently press on it to make sure it is firm but still has a bit of "give." Tap on it and listen for a solid sound. If it sounds hollow, it means that the fruit has dried out. Here are some tips for working with avocados.

STEP ONE: Cut the avocado in half. Generally, I like to first cut avocados open lengthwise, into two halves. Do this by inserting the blade of a knife at the top of the avocado and cutting down the middle until you reach the pit. At this point, turn the avocado on the knife, making your way around the pit, until the blade meets the initial cut that you made at the top of the fruit.

STEP TWO: Remove the skin. Peel the pitted half by gently removing the skin in large strips with your fingers. If necessary, you can use the tip of your knife to help get each strip started. Alternatively, you can scoop out the avocado

Roberto SANTIBAÑEZ

★ ★ ★ ★ ★ ★ ★ ★

PROFILE

Born and raised in Mexico City, Roberto Santibañez received his culinary training at the prestigious Cordon Bleu and Notre in Paris. Following an apprenticeship at La Bourgogne, he became the executive chef of the Henbury Estate in Cheshire, England. He then returned to Mexico City to cook at the private dining room of the Foreign Affairs Ministry and then at El Olivo, where he won praise for his blend of French and Mexican flavors. As chef-owner of El Sax, La Circunstancia, and Restobar Salamandra, Santibañez helped revitalize downtown Mexico City before arriving in the United States as executive chef at the award-winning Fonda San Miguel in Austin, Texas. He is now culinary director of Rosa Mexicano in New York City.

flesh directly from the skin with a large spoon, or carefully make three or four cuts down and across the flesh so that it can be scooped out in neat cubes.

STEP THREE: Remove the pit. To pit an avocado half, prick the pit with the tip of your knife, lodging it there. Work your knife back and forth to loosen the pit from all sides of the fruit, using an easy, twisting motion. The entire pit should lift out cleanly, leaving the flesh intact.

MORE CHEF'S SECRETS . . .

FM: How did you start cooking?
RS: My grandmother was an amazing dynamo of a woman who loved to travel and cook. She'd come back from trips with an armload of new recipes and invite me and my friends over for a daylong extravaganza of cooking and eating. That really got me hooked.

FM: Who were your role models?
RS: There are so many . . . I would certainly say Josefina Howard, Diana Kennedy, and Patricia Quintana—true matriarchs of Mexican cooking who introduced the world to what was then a "new" cuisine, paving the way for chefs like me.

FM: Pet peeve?
RS: Shortcuts in the kitchen. There's a reason why classical methods have been passed down for generations. For me, flavor must come first. I don't make any compromises.

ROBERTO SANTIBAÑEZ'S GUACAMOLE EN MOLCAJETE

To prepare guacamole in the most authentic way, use a *molcajete*—a traditional Mexican mortar and pestle made out of volcanic stone. But if a *molcajete* is not available, a small mixing bowl works just fine.

- 3 tablespoons chopped white onion, divided
- 1/2 teaspoon chopped serrano chiles
- 1 1/2 teaspoons finely chopped cilantro, divided
- 1/2 teaspoon salt
- 1 ripe Hass avocado, cut in half lengthwise and pitted
- 1 small vine-ripened tomato, chopped, with seeds and center removed

In a small bowl, thoroughly mash 1 tablespoon of the chopped onion, the serrano chile, 1/2 teaspoon cilantro, and the salt with the back of a wooden spoon until it becomes a juicy paste.

Cut into the flesh of each avocado half, making slits both down and across to form a grid. Scoop out the avocado from the skin and place it in the bowl with the onion paste. Stir thoroughly to coat with the paste. Add the remaining onion and cilantro, and the tomato. Gently fold to incorporate all the ingredients. Add more chopped chiles and salt to taste.

Serve with freshly made tortilla chips or corn tortillas.

Serves 2

Ryan HUGHES

HOW TO QUICKLY RIPEN FRUIT

★ ★ ★ ★ ★ ★ ★ ★ ★ ★ ★

I use apples to ripen other fruit. This works especially well in my restaurant kitchen when I need to ripen avocados or plantains. I place the unripe fruit on top of the case of apples, and in return, the ripening process is speeded twofold. This is also a good technique for the home kitchen because people who do not have access to locally and organically grown produce typically end up having to select from the unripe fruit and vegetables that are peddled in so many supermarkets.

STEP ONE: Place the fruit you would like to ripen in an ordinary brown paper bag along with an apple or two. Fruits, especially apples, give off a gas called ethylene as they ripen. Exposure to ethylene speeds the ripening of other fruits.

STEP TWO: Leave it on the kitchen counter overnight. In a relatively short time (usually by the next day), you will have a far superior, riper product than you bought.

MORE CHEF'S SECRETS . . .

FM: Favorite middle-of-the-night snack?
RH: Leftover Vietnamese.

FM: Screenplay about the restaurant business—what would you call it?
RH: *Who's on What?*

FM: Kitchen ritual?
RH: Every Saturday night, I torture the kitchen staff with *Hall & Oates' Greatest Hits*.

David CARMICHAEL

PROFILE

David Carmichael began his pastry career at the Barefoot Contessa in East Hampton, New York, while he was still in high school. A graduate of the Culinary Institute of America, Carmichael worked under François Payard in the pastry department of Le Bernardin, as well as at Restaurant Daniel, before becoming head pastry chef at Lutèce under André Soltner. After a short summer break to gather his thoughts and plan for the future, Carmichael, the 1998 winner of the annual Patisfrance U.S. Pastry Competition, became executive pastry chef at Oceana, where he's been plying his trade to rave reviews ever since.

HOW TO PEEL A PEACH

★ ★ ★ ★ ★ ★ ★ ★ ★ ★ ★ ★

Peaches are as hard to peel as tomatoes. Which made me think, hey, why not peel them the way you would a ripe Roma or summer beefsteak? However, the peaches need to be very ripe for this peeling technique to work well (if the peaches are not ripe, the skin won't pull away from the flesh). To choose ripe peaches, lightly touch the surface of the fruit; it should give a little bit.

STEP ONE: Fill a 3-quart saucepan with 2^1/2 quarts of water and bring to a rolling boil. At the same time, fill a bowl with water and add several ice cubes.

STEP TWO: Using a sharp paring knife, make an "X" opposite the stem end of each peach. Don't attempt to peel too many peaches at once—I recommend working with four at a time.

STEP THREE: Drop the peaches in the boiling water. Count to 14. Using a slotted spoon, immediately remove the peaches to the ice bath to shock (stop the cooking process with the drastic temperature change).

STEP FOUR: Remove the skin. When the peaches are cooled, gently rub the skin away from each peach with your fingers. Now they are perfect for serving à la mode.

MORE CHEF'S SECRETS . . .

FM: Do you have a good luck kitchen ritual?
DC: I always wear my chef's hat, which looks like a white beret. I don't work as well without it, and I can only buy it in England, so whenever I'm there, I buy tons.

FM: How tall can a dessert be before it topples over?
DC: I can make a dessert that's 5 feet tall, if I want to. Just glue it with caramel. But for a regular restaurant sort of dessert, if the dessert pokes the diner in the eye, you've gone too high.

FM: Who or what is the culinary mother of invention?
DC: Childhood memories—a lot of chefs are inspired by childhood memories.

Emily LUCHETTI

PROFILE

With a B.A. in sociology from Denison University, Emily Luchetti moved to New York City to pursue a career in the culinary arts. She worked at the New York Restaurant School, David Leiderman's Manhattan Market, and the Silver Palate before joining the opening team of Stars Restaurant in San Francisco, where she started as a line cook and worked her way up to lunch sous chef. In 1987, she became the pastry chef at Stars and co-owner (with Jeremiah Tower) of StarBake, a retail bakery. Luchetti, the 2004 James Beard Award winner for Best Pastry Chef, is now the executive pastry chef of Farallon Restaurant in San Francisco. She contributed to *The All-New All-Purpose Joy of Cooking* and has written several books, including *Stars Desserts*, *Four-Star Desserts*, and *A Passion for Desserts*.

HOW TO CARE FOR STRAWBERRIES

★ ★ ★ ★ ★ ★ ★ ★ ★ ★ ★ ★

With all fruits, but especially strawberries, careful selection at the market is key. Choose strawberries that have a perfumed aroma (strawberries that are fragrant generally also taste better). Always check the bottom of a strawberry basket before purchasing; the prettiest ones are often placed on top, and there may be underripe or spoiled berries underneath. Luckily, the green mesh plastic basket makes inspection easy. Here's the best way to take care of your strawberries once you get them home from the market.

★ **Store strawberries in a single layer.** If you are not going to eat the strawberries the day you purchase them, remove them from the basket and place them in a single layer on a tray or plate. Leaving the strawberries in their container causes them to deteriorate much more quickly, and one bad berry will ruin the others.

★ **Keep strawberries in the refrigerator, but let them sit at room temperature for 15 minutes before serving to take the chill off.** Eating strawberries that are too cold deprives you of their fullest flavor and fragrance.

★ **Wash strawberries the day you plan to eat them.** There is a right and a wrong way to wash strawberries. Don't hull or cut the berries before washing, so they won't get waterlogged. Never wash strawberries prior to the day you plan to eat them. Fill a large bowl with cold water and gently place the berries in the water; swish them around with your hands. This allows any dirt or sand to sink to the bottom of the bowl. Lift the berries from the bowl and place them on a clean towel.

★ **If you're going to add sugar to the strawberries, wait until just before serving.**
If I am serving berries at a party and want to do as much work as possible in advance, I slice them ahead of time but wait until just before I serve them to add any sugar. Strawberries, unlike raspberries or blueberries, release their own juices when sliced. Adding sugar hastens that process. Always taste your strawberries before adding sugar—strawberries picked at the height of the season often don't need additional sugar; they are sweet and juicy enough on their own.

MORE CHEF'S SECRETS . . .

FM: What is your most prized kitchen possession?
EL: A KitchenAid 5-quart standing mixer.

FM: What is your idea of culinary heaven?
EL: All the pastries I want to bake and eat without getting full. And no calories.

FM: Culinary hell?
EL: A customer who wants a sugar-free/fat-free/gluten-free dessert.

Roxanne KLEIN

PROFILE

Fifth-generation Californian and organic, living-foods proponent Roxanne Klein has emerged as one of America's hottest chefs—no small feat, especially considering that every dish she creates is raw. After graduating from the California Culinary Academy and working her way through many internationally recognized kitchens, Klein opened her eponymous restaurant in San Francisco, vaulting to the forefront of the newest culinary genre and garnering recognition from virtually every major national and international publication that covers fine dining. Klein has also applied her zeal for creating new recipes to a living-foods cookbook, *RAW*, coauthored with six-time James Beard Award—winning chef Charlie Trotter.

HOW TO GET COCONUT WATER OUT OF A BABY COCONUT

Coconut water is different from coconut milk, as the water is found only in baby coconuts. We use coconut water at Roxanne's as a refreshing drink and as an ingredient in some of our dishes. Water from young coconuts not only is delicious, but also is a wonderful source of electrolytes and is a natural blood purifier.

Even after the hard outer shell is removed, coconuts can be difficult to open. The task is made more difficult if you are trying to preserve the water. It is also very easy to ruin a good knife in the process. The method I devised allows you to get the water from the coconut easily without using a knife or a machete. It involves using the pointed end of a knife-sharpening steel, which is easy and safe—even my children can open their own coconuts.

STEP ONE: Choose the best possible coconut.
Young coconuts have a white outer husk, which is different from the hard, mature brown coconuts. Look for one that is pure white and free of any brown spots. Check the bottom of the coconut (the flat side) for any discoloration, which may indicate improper storage or aged and inferior coconut water. Young coconuts should always be kept refrigerated.

STEP TWO: Place the coconut with the flat side on a work surface, so the slightly pointed end faces up.

STEP THREE: Position the end of a knife steel approximately 1 inch off the top, center, peaked portion of the coconut.

STEP FOUR: With your other hand, grab the side of the coconut. Lift up while simultaneously pressing the steel into the coconut as you tap the steel down toward the work surface (at right). It will take one or two taps to puncture a hole in the top.

STEP FIVE: To drain the water from the coconut, repeat the procedure to make a second hole. The water will come out very easily. It's ready to use without being strained. Chill it for a refreshing drink. If you want to drink directly from coconut, simply use a straw at this point, and enjoy.

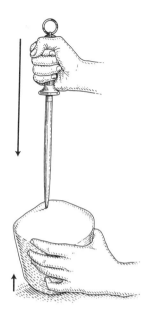

MORE CHEF'S SECRETS . . .

FM: Most prized kitchen utensil?
RK: Mandoline.

FM: Best food market ever?
RK: In addition to some spectacular markets in Paris and Florence, the San Francisco Ferry Plaza Farmers' Market is my favorite.

FM: Culinary hero?
RK: Julia Child. I grew up watching her shows.

CHAPTER FIVE

★ ★ ★ ★

RICE, BEANS, & PASTA

Scott CONANT

HOW TO BOOST THE FLAVOR OF PASTA

★ ★ ★ ★ ★ ★ ★ ★ ★ ★ ★ ★

Pasta is so misunderstood in the United States. This traditional Italian technique ensures that the pasta will be properly cooked al dente. Since cooking water absorbs the pasta's starches, when the water is used in a quick pan sauce, it gives excellent texture and depth to the finished pasta dish. Likewise, when you finish cooking the pasta in the sauce, the pasta has time to absorb the flavors and is therefore much tastier than if served with sauce simply spooned over it.

STEP ONE: Only partially cook dry pasta. In a pot of abundantly salted boiling water, cook dry pasta for only half or three-quarters of the recommended time. The timing depends on the brand, shape, and size—I recommend reading the package instructions. Tasting pasta is the best indicator of doneness, and in this case, it should be too hard to eat, but soft enough that you can taste the dough.

STEP TWO: Add the semi-cooked pasta to a pan sauce. Using a slotted spoon (for shaped pasta) or tongs (for spaghetti), remove the partially cooked pasta from the water, reserving the water for later use. Add the pasta to the pan of sauce. For example, when I cook spaghetti with clams, I sauté the clams in olive oil, garlic, and white wine, and as they open and release their liquid, I transfer the semi-cooked pasta straight from the pot of boiling water into the pan with the clams.

STEP THREE: Adjust the thickness of the sauce by adding the reserved water. Finish cooking the pasta in the *cuisson* (cooking liquid). Add the reserved water to adjust the thickness of the sauce. Reduce by simmering and season as necessary, bearing in mind that the pasta water you are adding to the pan is heavily salted. If you reduce it too much, the dish can get too salty.

MORE CHEF'S SECRETS . . .

FM: Do you have a kitchen routine?
SC: I come in, drink three double espressos, and then I walk into the cooler and take a mental inventory so that I know what I'm facing for the day. Then I delegate, expedite, the works—including checking the reservations.

FM: What could you eat over and over and never get bored?
SC: Mortadella, Skippy Extra Chunky Peanut Butter, and sea urchin. But not all at once.

FM: What's your favorite food market?
SC: Chelsea Market in Manhattan has the best variety.

Jennifer NEWBURY

HOW TO MAKE PERFECT PASTA FROM SCRATCH

★ ★ ★ ★ ★ ★ ★ ★ ★ ★ ★ ★

I like to use a little white wine in my pasta dough. Not only does it add flavor and aroma to the dough, but the alcohol in the wine evaporates a bit so the pasta is firmer than an all-egg dough. I still use quite a few whole eggs for tenderness and richness, but the white wine adds a nuance that leaves the pasta aromatic. I also use "oo" flour, a finely milled semolina flour made specifically for pasta, because it gives a resilient texture with no gluey-ness, and then I add some medium-ground semolina for texture.

STEP ONE: Make a batch of my favorite pasta dough (see recipe on page 135) and get out your pasta machine.

STEP TWO: Divide the dough into workable portions. It takes the same amount of time to roll a little dough as it does to roll a larger quantity, so work with the biggest sheet of dough you can properly manage. Eventually the sheet should be wide enough that it presses lightly against the sides of the machine, which will ensure a smooth edge and pretty noodles all the way across. This usually means dividing the dough in half, depending on the size of the machine you are using.

STEP THREE: Roll the dough through the pasta machine, twice through each setting (Figure A). The secret to perfect pasta dough is how you roll it through the machine. Pass the dough through each setting (until it is as wide as it needs to be) two times. On my machine, this means starting at the number 10 setting (the widest) and working down to the number 7. Each machine is slightly different, but I suggest starting with these numbers until you get the hang of the rolling process. Then you can make adjustments, bearing in mind that pasta swells when cooked and you always want to roll it thinner than what you are looking for in a finished dish.

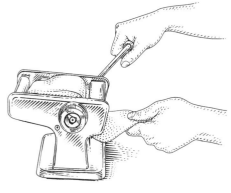

Figure A

STEP FOUR: Fold the dough and run it back through the machine again. When the dough is long enough to fold into thirds, fold each end in once, like a letter before you place it in an envelope (Figure B). You will then have a seamed edge as well as two open ends. Return the machine to the widest setting and pass the folded dough through, leading with one of the open edges (Figure C). Repeat this folding process three times. After the last pass through the machine, continue to roll the dough to the desired thickness (this depends on the shape of the pasta you want) by passing the pasta sheet through each setting two times. Folding the dough before passing it

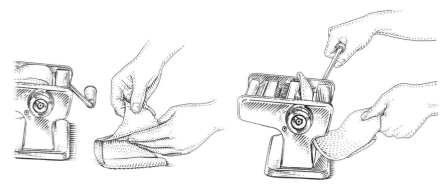

Figure B   Figure C

through (called turning the dough) means it gets uniformly stretched, so that if you are making noodles, they will be flat and smooth instead of kinky. With that, the pasta is ready to make into shapes.

MORE CHEF'S SECRETS . . .

FM: Favorite pizza combination?
JN: Ricotta salata (dry ricotta), arugula, and white anchovies, though not necessarily together.

FM: Culinary good luck charm?
JN: A kitchen witch that hangs over the sink.

FM: Best advice for a home cook?
JN: Don't be married to a recipe; add a flourish that makes it yours.

JENNIFER NEWBURY'S
PERFECT PASTA DOUGH

3 cups "oo" pasta flour (semolina)
1 cup medium-ground semolina flour
1 tablespoon salt
6 eggs
$^1/_4$ cup white wine

With a wooden spoon, combine the "oo" pasta flour, medium-ground semolina flour, and salt in the bowl of a heavy-duty mixer fitted with a dough hook. In a separate bowl, whisk together the eggs and wine.

With the mixer running on its lowest speed, add the egg mixture to the dry ingredients in a steady stream. The dry ingredients will come together and form a ball, leaving no dough stuck to the sides of the bowl. The mixer will be working hard and making the noise to prove it; not to worry. If the dough is too sticky, you may have to add a little more "oo" flour until the bowl is clean.

Knead the dough (with the mixer) until it is smooth and of the same consistency all the way through. Knead the ball a few times by hand to check the texture. The dough may feel slightly warm from the work of the mixer. Cover the dough ball with an inverted mixing bowl and let it rest for at least 20 minutes before rolling it out for pasta.

Makes enough dough for about 8 servings of pasta

Barbara LYNCH

★ ★ ★ ★ ★ ★ ★

HOW TO MAKE GNOCCHI THE IRISH-ITALIAN WAY

★ ★ ★ ★ ★ ★ ★ ★ ★ ★ ★ ★

Everyone always wonders how an Irish girl from Boston learned to make good pasta. I didn't grow up making gnocchi, but potatoes—well, potatoes I know. Making gnocchi by hand is stupidly easy, and ensuring that the gnocchi are lighter than air rather than leaden potato dumplings lies in one tip: Chill your riced potatoes. They'll absorb much less flour when cool, which will keep them fluffy. And practice. The more often you make these, the easier it becomes.

STEP ONE: Prepare the potatoes. Boil 2 pounds (about 3 large) russet potatoes in salted water. Leave the skin on the potatoes—cooking them with the skin on prevents them from getting water-logged, which can weigh them down. When tender, remove them from the water, remove the skin, and push them through a ricer. Then the key: Spread the riced potatoes on a sheet pan and refrigerate until cool.

STEP TWO: Have ¹/₂ cup of flour handy. Sprinkle about half of it over the riced potatoes; then use your hands to gather them into a mound. Make a well in the center of the mound, and in a separate bowl whisk together 2 eggs and a teaspoon of salt. Pour the egg mixture into the well. Use your fingertips to gently massage the egg into the potato (Figure A). Don't go crazy—you're not kneading dough here! It will be sticky. Add just a little bit of flour at a time, easing it in with your fingertips until the dough is no longer sticky. Do not add more flour than you need—you don't have to use it all. Too much flour leads to leaden gnocchi.

STEP THREE: Roll out the gnocchi. Gather the potato mixture into a ball (Figure B) and divide it into four equal pieces. Roll the pieces into long, thin snakes (Figure C). Cut the snakes into pieces a little larger than your thumbnail. Roll the pieces into balls, and then roll the balls across a gnocchi board (Figure D) or the tines of a fork. (With the fork facing tines down, roll the balls along the rounded back, pressing to make ridges that will hold the sauce.)

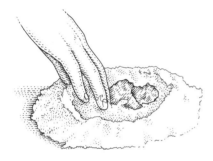

Figure A

Figure B

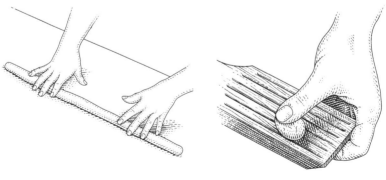

Figure C

Figure D

STEP FOUR: Cook the gnocchi in boiling salted water until they float to the top, about 2 minutes. Serve right away, or run the cooked gnocchi under cool water until cold; then freeze.

MORE CHEF'S SECRETS . . .

FM: Favorite junk food?
BL: Cheez-Its. I have an addiction. People know how much I love them, so now even the most discerning friends or clients keep a box on hand if they know I'm coming over.

FM: Favorite cookbook?
BL: *Le Grand Livre de Cuisine d'Alain Ducasse.* It's a huge encyclopedia of his recipes—a huge book. It probably weighs 15 pounds. It's unbelievably comprehensive, and I totally respect his food.

FM: Favorite non-food job?
BL: Well, I'm not sure it was my "favorite," but before I started cooking, I worked as a bookie. That was interesting.

HOW TO MAKE
SHORTCUT RAVIOLI

★ ★ ★ ★ ★ ★ ★ ★ ★ ★ ★ ★ ★

Few people have the time or energy to make fresh ravioli at home these days, so I'll let you in on a secret: Use wonton skins instead of making pasta dough. Restaurants do this all the time, since the daunting prospect of forming hundreds or thousands of these little dumplings from scratch might send any number of chefs into early retirement (although, strangely, I rather enjoy it). Here's what to do.

STEP ONE: Purchase wonton skins or gyoza wraps (they're similar to wonton skins, but round and a bit thicker) from the produce section of the supermarket.

STEP TWO: Lay your "pasta" sheets out in a line, working with eight at a time. Brush the exposed side of each sheet with beaten egg, lightly but thoroughly, and place a dollop of a filling you enjoy in the center. Top each loosely with a second "pasta" sheet.

STEP THREE: Cut out the ravioli. Using a round form just large enough to encase your filling—a juice glass, the back (not the cutting edge) of a cookie cutter, or whatever you prefer—gently press down over the filling so that it is tightly encased, working to push out any air pockets. With a cookie cutter or even the tip of a paring knife, cut around the newly formed ravioli in whatever shape you desire, then transfer the

Jay
MURRAY

PROFILE

By the time he was in the fourth grade, cooking had become an obsession for Jay Murray, whose parents ran a cooking school in Darien, Connecticut. Murray, who learned his craft through years of exposure, attended college to become a writer but couldn't resist the call of the kitchen. After honing his skills under Gabino Sotelino at Chicago's Un Grand Café, Murray made his name at New England's top inns, first at the Blantyre and then as executive chef of Silks at the acclaimed Stonehedge Inn. Executive chef of Boston's Grill 23 since 1998, Murray has seen the restaurant receive Top American Restaurant, Top Steakhouse, and Top Seafood Restaurant from the Zagat Survey, as well as being named one of America's Top 10 Steakhouses by *Town & Country*.

ravioli to a lightly floured surface to await cooking. One word of advice: The bigger your ravioli, the fewer you need to make; I always make them giant, so that two fill the bill for a meal.

STEP FOUR: Prepare or freeze. Once all are formed, they are ready to boil, steam, fry, or sauté. Or, if you prefer, they can be kept in the freezer and cooked from frozen whenever the mood arises.

MORE CHEF'S SECRETS . . .

FM: First thing you do when you get to work?
JM: Check all my phone and e-mail messages.

FM: Last thing you do before you leave?
JM: Bring my butcher a Stoli on the rocks with an olive and a twist for all he's had to go through.

FM: Kitchen anthem?
JM: Anything from Bowie's "Lady Stardust" to the Sugar Hill Gang's "Rapper's Delight," unless, of course, there's a Red Sox game on the radio.

HOW TO KEEP A WHITE RISOTTO WHITE

★ ★ ★ ★ ★ ★ ★ ★ ★ ★ ★ ★ ★

When preparing a white risotto, I want to sweat the onions properly, which means cooking them over low heat for 7 to 10 minutes not only to soften them and extract their flavor but also to keep them from browning, which would discolor the risotto. If I had the time to stand there and constantly stir, there would be no problem, but life in the kitchen can become very distracting. Multitasking is a must! Instead of waiting until the onions are translucent before adding the wine, I take this shortcut.

STEP ONE: Gather and prepare all the ingredients; then add the onions to the pan. After I *brunoise* (finely dice) my onions, I place them along with a little olive oil in a large *rondo* (a heavy wide pan that allows for even evaporation of cooking liquid; substitute a large skillet with straight sides or wide stockpot) on a high heat setting. I make sure that all my ingredients are ready to go. Then I open a bottle of dry white wine and a box of Arborio rice. (Typically I open one bottle of wine for each 2-pound box.) I also have chicken stock and some salt and pepper on hand.

STEP TWO: Cool off the pan with a splash of wine to avoid browning the onions. As the onions release their liquid and start to simmer, the pan will become hot (you will notice a metallic smell). I add a splash of white wine to cool off

Alex A. FREIJ

★ ★ ★ ★ ★ ★ ★ ★ ★ ★ ★

PROFILE

After cooking his way around the world and through the notable kitchens of Alain Ducasse, Jean-Georges Vongerichten, and the late Jean-Louis Palladin, Alex A. Freij, a graduate of the California Culinary Academy, has settled down at Industry (Food), a self-styled chef's club where he serves an eclectic menu of "New American cuisine at neighborhood prices." Freij, executive chef and owner, chose New York's stylish East Village because the "vibe" matches the character of the restaurant he always wanted to open—downtown spirit mixed with a worldly sophistication.

the pan. This process is very important because it will impart a little bit of the wine's flavor and stabilize the heat in the pan so the onions do not brown. Repeat this process twice until the onions are translucent.

STEP THREE: Gradually add all the rice to the pan and pour in any remaining wine. As you add the rice, you will begin to smell a nutty aroma. After the wine has evaporated, that nutty smell will dissipate. At this time, follow a standard risotto recipe from one of the Italian cooking masters like Marcella Hazan, adding the hot chicken stock and stirring until the risotto is cooked.

MORE CHEF'S SECRETS . . .

FM: If you weren't in this industry (food), which one would you be in?
AF: Advertising. I am a really creative guy, and it would be a fun job. Not only would I be able to share my creativity, I could also influence consumers to purchase products.

FM: Who are the chefs you think have done the most to set industry standards?
AF: As a chef you must be ingenious and artistic, and most important, you must know what the people want to eat and how to present it to them. Wolfgang Puck and Todd English have done this.

FM: When chefs get together, what do they talk about?
AF: When I get together with other chefs we usually talk about other chefs, of course, crazy cooking stories, good old times and past experiences we have had together, and hostesses.

HOW TO USE BACON TO ITS BEST ADVANTAGE WHEN COOKING BEANS

★ ★ ★ ★ ★ ★ ★ ★ ★ ★ ★ ★

John MANION

★ ★ ★ ★ ★ ★ ★ ★ ★ ★

I have to say that bacon is my most trusted ingredient in the kitchen. It can really make just about anything taste better, with a smokiness and richness not found elsewhere. There are three elements to using bacon as a cornerstone of my cooking—especially with beans—that make it irreplaceable. First, the cure; this allows me to add a deep salt/sweet note that develops at the very onset of the cooking process. The second element is the smoke, which will also impart a deep, subtle, almost sublime flavor. The third and probably most important element, for me, is the fat. In fact, to cook beans without pork fat is an insult to the beans—almost a culinary sin. I have a ton of loyal vegetarian customers for whom I make every effort to prepare wonderful, pork fat–free dishes. Beans are not one of them. Here's how I do it.

STEP ONE: Render the bacon in a saucepan big enough to hold the beans and their cooking liquid. We use slab bacon at the restaurant, so we reserve the ends and odd pieces for cooking beans. Make sure the pieces are cut into a uniform size and shape, such as a $1/8$-inch dice, so that they cook uniformly. Start with a heavy bottomed, 8-quart stockpot. Place the room-temperature bacon into a room-temperature stockpot and turn the flame up to medium. While it may seem

PROFILE

Midwestern-born John Manion moved to São Paulo as a boy, and the exotic ingredients and unfamiliar smells left their mark. After five years steeped in Brazil's kitchen culture, Manion returned to the United States and began his culinary career as a dishwasher when he was thirteen. After graduating from Marquette University, Manion attended the Culinary School of Kendall College in Chicago, training under Dean Zanella at Grappa. He was opening chef at Savannah's, named one of the Best New Restaurants by *Chicago* magazine, and also worked with Nuevo Latino master Michael Cordua at Churrascos (also in Chicago). Now co-owner and executive chef of Mas in Chicago, Manion is known for food rooted in the peasant cultures, something he credits to his Brazilian kitchen childhood.

counterintuitive not to preheat the pot (as in every other recipe you have ever read), this gentle cooking method will coax the fat out of the bacon without scorching the pan and without spitting hot grease at you. It should take about 10 minutes for the bacon to render its fat. At this point, remove the bacon and let rest. Now here's the sick part—do not drain the fat. Leave it in the pot.

STEP TWO: Sauté the beans in the rendered bacon fat. With the bacon fat still in the pot, add 3 cups of Great Northern beans (rinsed and picked through; you may be surprised at how many little pebbles you find) and a head of whole peeled garlic cloves. Sauté for 3 to 4 minutes, scraping any crust from the bottom of the pan as you turn the beans gently. After 3 minutes, the beans should glisten, and you will start to smell the garlic. (While it may fly in the face of convention, you really don't need to pre-soak the beans. I've been eating and cooking beans most of my life and here is my opinion: Soaking your beans does nothing. They don't cook faster. They don't taste better. You still run the risk of embarrassing flatulence. Don't bother soaking your beans.)

STEP THREE: Deglaze the pot. At this juncture, add a splash of cider vinegar to the pot. Keep cooking, scraping the bottom of the pot with a wooden spoon (all those caramelized bits equal flavor), and make sure all of the vinegar is evaporated.

STEP FOUR: Add the salt, bacon, liquid, and aromatics. Now add salt—2 tablespoons should do the trick. Put in the bacon and stir, stir, stir. Pour in enough hot liquid to cover the beans by about 4 inches. I would recommend chicken stock or a light pork stock, but if bouillon cubes are your only answer, use plain water instead. Add 1 bay leaf and about 6 sprigs of thyme tied tightly, bring to a boil, and immediately turn it down to a low simmer. (Thyme, bay leaf, and Great Northerns are a match made in heaven. For black beans, I would use either cilantro or epazote.)

STEP FIVE: Be patient. The longer the beans cook, the more tender they will be, and the more the flavors we have added (i.e., *bacon*) will be imparted into the beans. You may need to add more liquid during the cooking process.

STEP SIX: Taste. We simmer our beans for about 2 hours, but there is no way to actually give you a time frame. You need to taste them to know, so taste. When they taste good to you, they are done. Drain and serve immediately. If you think you deserve it, douse them with a little white truffle oil.

MORE CHEF'S SECRETS . . .

FM: Do you have a kitchen ritual?
JM: Lists. My kitchen ritual is really just one big list. I begin each morning with an espresso and my first list.

FM: A culinary good luck charm?
JM: I really don't believe in luck, other than the fact that you make your own luck every day. Hard work, focus, and staying true to who you are is really the only good luck charm one can really count on.

FM: A piece of advice you like to give your new cooks?
JM: Listen to what people are willing to tell you because you never know what you might learn.

CHAPTER SIX

★ ★ ★ ★

KITCHEN STAPLES

James
PETERSON

PROFILE

In 1975, after studying chemistry at UC Berkeley, James Peterson set out for India in search of a guru. Although spiritual enlightenment was elusive, a stop in Paris on his way back from Calcutta revealed Peterson's true calling: gastronomy. After attending Le Cordon Bleu and working with George Blanc at Chez La Mère Blanc, Peterson opened the critically acclaimed Le Petit Robert in New York City in 1980. By 1984, ready to share his culinary expertise, he left the restaurant business and went about teaching and writing. Peterson is the author of eight books, primarily single-subject compendiums such as *Sauces: Classical and Contemporary Sauce Making*, that not only win awards (like the IACP Cookbook Award and James Beard Cookbook of the Year) but make good cooks of us all.

HOW TO INTENSIFY THE FLAVOR OF SAUCE

When making a sauce that requires broth, intensify flavor by reducing the broth with the trimmings of whatever you are serving; for example, use the trimmings from a beef roast to enhance the beef broth for the sauce.

STEP ONE: Brown the trimmings with coarsely chopped aromatic vegetables (like carrots and onions or leeks) in a small amount of butter or oil. Cook gently so the trimmings and vegetables release their juices, allowing the sugar in the vegetables to caramelize (without burning) on the bottom of the saucepan or pot.

STEP TWO: Add a small amount—say 1/2 cup—of broth, and bring to a low boil until the broth completely disappears. The trimmings and vegetables will continue to caramelize, and there will be a brown film left on the bottom of the pan. Repeat this process as many times as you want—once is good; three times is even better.

STEP THREE: After the caramelizing is finished, add just enough broth to make the sauce you need. Stir and simmer gently with the caramelized trimmings and vegetables for about 5 minutes. Strain. Although long simmering provides body, most people don't realize that broth loses flavor when cooked too long. The ideal here is to take your long-simmered broth and then use it during the caramelizing to intensify your sauce.

MORE CHEF'S SECRETS . . .

FM: Cooking—art or science?

JP: First, cooking is a craft, and of course, a science, in the sense that hypotheses can be tested and verified. Defining it as art is trickier. However, if art is the expression of a vision through the medium of a craft, then cooking—used to create beauty both visual and gustatory—clearly makes it.

FM: What is the best kitchen advice you've ever gotten?

JP: Use only the best ingredients and treat them in such a way as to underline their intrinsic nature—the ingredients will tell you how to cook them (or not) if you listen to them.

FM: The best advice you've ever given?

JP: The same as I was given. And to my students: Read! Read! Read! Try to study in a different country. Cooking is a reflection of culture and traditions, not just clever recipes.

Norman
VAN AKEN

HOW TO MAKE
A PAN SAUCE

★ ★ ★ ★ ★ ★ ★ ★ ★ ★ ★ ★

One of my most valuable *trucs* is the value of acidity (like wine, vinegar, and citrus juices) in the overall flavor of foods. The choice of which to use grows out of the geographical roots of the food (like rice wine vinegar for food with Asian roots). Two of my favorites are versatile Spanish sherry vinegar, which works whether I'm making a meat-based reduction, a nut oil vinaigrette, a butter sauce, or a simple marinade, and fresh citrus juices, because they easily cross geographical zones, providing a tangy dagger of flavor. Here's how you can make acidity work for you when you are making a pan sauce (a simple, natural combination enhanced by bits of food and caramelized juices left in the pan).

STEP ONE: When you are finished pan grilling (or oven roasting), remove the meat, poultry, or fish to a warm platter and cover loosely with foil.

STEP TWO: Pour excess fat from the pan (leaving a fine film on the bottom) and place the pan over low heat.

STEP THREE: Add chopped shallots and/or minced garlic and stir with a wooden spoon until softened and lightly colored, about a minute or two.

STEP FOUR: Use an acidic liquid to loosen the

fond **from the bottom of the pan.** Add several tablespoons of wine, vinegar, or citrus juice and allow the liquid to bubble up, loosening the browned bits of food (called *fond*) from the bottom of the pan. Allow the liquid to reduce slightly (it will appear syrupy).

STEP FIVE: Finish off the sauce and serve. Add a drop of olive oil or a small knob of unsalted butter, swirling the pan to incorporate the fat into the liquid. When the sauce is smooth, pour over the roasted meat, poultry, or fish, and serve.

MORE CHEF'S SECRETS . . .

FM: What is the greatest American food city (other than your own)?
NVA: New York City.

FM: What is your idea of a culinary splurge?
NVA: Tin of osetra caviar and toasted brioche.

FM: What is the best advice you can give to someone who wants to open a restaurant?
NVA: Work in as many very-good-to-great restaurants as you can for a minimum of 10 years. Don't rush yourself. Wait until you're about thirty-five years old before taking on the nearly "monastic" life one must succumb to for several years to make your dream a success.

Paul
KAHAN

★ ★ ★ ★

PROFILE

Paul Kahan, a 1999 *Food & Wine* Best New Chef, grew up working in his father's delicatessen and smokehouse. He did a brief post-collegiate stint as a computer scientist before taking a job in the kitchen of Erwin Dreschler's Metropolis, where he quickly realized his life's passion. With a deep appreciation for local, organic ingredients, Kahan developed relationships with many midwestern farmers, integrating their offerings into seasonal dishes. In 1997, Kahan joined Donnie Madia to launch Blackbird, where his commitment to local ingredients landed the restaurant on *Gourmet* magazine's 2001 list of the country's 50 Best Restaurants. Kahan is the 2004 award winner for James Beard Best Chef of the Midwest, and Blackbird was the winner of the James Beard Foundation's Best Restaurant Design Award in 2002.

HOW TO DOUBLE-FLAVOR
A CLASSIC *JUS*

★ ★ ★ ★ ★ ★ ★ ★ ★ ★ ★ ★

A classic *jus* is really just a simple sauce made from reduced stock. At the restaurant, we always use an appropriate stock, such as squab stock for a squab dish, and then incorporate the different aspects of the dish into the stock and sauce so that the dish stays more intense. Our goal is to intensify each individual ingredient so it is fully realized and adds as much to the dish as possible. This double-flavor technique evokes a traditional Mexican sauce-making technique I learned from Rick Bayless at Topolobampo and means adding a flavor ingredient to the sauce during the reduction stage and again during the finishing stage. Here's how to do it.

STEP ONE: Make the *jus*. Sweat (cover and cook) a *mirepoix* (a mixture of diced root vegetables, typically celery, onion, and carrots) and *bouquet garni* (a traditional flavoring agent for soups and stews: parsley, bay leaf, and thyme tied together

with kitchen twine or placed in a muslin spice bag) in a saucepan, add an appropriate liquor (such as brandy for sour cherries), and reduce it to a syrupy consistency. Add the flavor-boosting ingredient (examples of what I use at the restaurant are pitted whole sour cherries and apricots, fresh herbs, or star anise) and the relevant stock. Reduce this over medium heat until the desired consistency is achieved. If the ingredients are all soft, combine in a blender, purée, and strain through a fine-mesh strainer. The result is the *jus*.

STEP TWO: When you are ready to serve, deglaze the roasting pan with the *jus* (pour off excess fat and add the *jus* to loosen bits of meat and caramelized cooking juices from the bottom of the pan) and add more of the flavor-boosting ingredient (such as pitted sour cherries).

STEP THREE: To increase body and flavor, add a knob of butter or a drizzle of olive oil and stir vigorously with a spoon while the *jus* is heating. Season to taste before serving.

MORE CHEF'S SECRETS . . .

FM: Favorite holiday meal?
PK: Oddly enough for this nice Jewish boy, the answer is Easter dinner at my wife's family's house. Her dad makes Polish sausage and puts it on the table with rye bread, feta cheese, and fresh horseradish. It is just a simple, delicious meal.

FM: Most comfortable shoes to wear in the kitchen?
PK: Birkenstock rubber clogs.

FM: Have a good luck kitchen charm?
PK: No, not really. If anything, my Minuso knives.

Pierre SCHAEDELIN

PROFILE

Pierre Schaedelin's passion for food began in his childhood in Alsace, near the French-German border. Schaedelin, who liked to make cakes, asked his grandmother to buy him a chef's hat, a tiny toque that his mother still keeps as a keepsake of her son's rapid ascent into the upper echelon of the culinary world. His international career stretches from the famed Auberge de L'ill in Illhaeusern, Alsace, France, where he was mentored by chef/owner Paul Haeberlin, to working under Alain Ducasse at Le Louis XV in the Hotel de Paris, Monaco. Shortly after Schaedelin took over the $3 million kitchen at New York's luxurious Le Cirque 2000, *Crain's New York* gave the new chef a four-star review for "coaxing maximum intensity from each fine, fresh ingredient."

HOW TO MAKE PERFECT GOLDEN CHICKEN CONSOMMÉ

★ ★ ★ ★ ★ ★ ★ ★ ★ ★ ★ ★

Traditional consommé (an adaptable clarified or clear broth that can be served hot or cold) preparation calls for egg whites and ground chicken; this easier method saves those steps and still imparts a rich color.

STEP ONE: Cut 2 chickens lengthwise and put them in a large, deep pot. Cover them with cold water and bring to a boil. Boil for 1 minute and then transfer the pot to the sink, running cold water directly over the chickens until they are chilled. Clean and dry the chickens and discard the water.

STEP TWO: Prepare the onions. Cut 3 onions in half and place them cut-side down on aluminum foil over high heat until burnt.

STEP THREE: Combine the ingredients in the same pot in which you cooked the chickens. Put 2 gallons of cold water in the pot and then add the chickens, 3 carrots cut in half, half a celery stalk, half a stalk of celeriac, and the burnt onions. The onions will give your consommé a beautiful golden color (don't worry, they won't give it a bad taste).

STEP FOUR: Slow-simmer everything together for a minimum of 1¹/2 hours. With this method, scum and grease will easily rise to the surface for skimming, which you should do every few minutes. Be careful to never let it come to a boil; only allow it to simmer slowly. One boil would automatically incorporate all the grease into the liquid, and it would no longer be clear.

STEP FIVE: After cooking, pass the mixture gently through cheesecloth. Reserve the chicken and vegetables, dice them, and add to the consommé as a garnish.

MORE CHEF'S SECRETS . . .

FM: Best kitchen advice you've ever gotten?
PS: Follow your instincts.

FM: Favorite food city other than your own?
PS: Paris.

FM: Piece of equipment you can't do without?
PS: A hand blender.

David McMILLAN

PROFILE

David McMillan, executive chef of Dallas's stellar Nana Grill in the Wyndham Anatole Hotel, studied fine arts and sculpture at Boston University before a stay in Europe set him on a culinary course. A former *commis* at Caffe Konig in Baden-Baden, one of Germany's finest resorts, McMillan has worked with some of Europe's most prestigious wine châteaux, including Petrus and Pontet-Canet. Stateside, McMillan was executive chef at Beverly Hills's Peninsula Hotel. As partner and executive chef of Legacy Restaurant, he presided over what *Los Angeles* magazine proclaimed one of the 10 Best New Restaurants in L.A.

HOW TO MAKE A PERFECT VINAIGRETTE

★ ★ ★ ★ ★ ★ ★ ★ ★ ★ ★ ★ ★

Poorly made vinaigrettes and salad dressings have always been one of my pet peeves—all oil on top and vinegar on the bottom, refusing to stay mixed long enough to pour on your salad. The trick to correcting this problem is to use a stabilizer that will become an integral part of the dressing, or, at least, a bona fide flavor component. One of my favorites is roasted tomato. It creates a velvety texture and rich flavor in a naturally stable vinaigrette that won't separate.

STEP ONE: Mix the ingredients. For about 2^1/2 cups of vinaigrette, toss ^{1}/2 cup assorted small tomatoes (like cherry or teardrop) with 2 sliced shallots, a pinch of coarse salt, a pinch of ground black pepper, several sprigs of fresh herbs, a splash of balsamic or Spanish sherry vinegar, and a splash of a good-quality olive oil.

STEP TWO: Spread on a sheet pan and roast in a preheated 300°F oven until the tomatoes "melt" (soften) and caramelize a bit (turn slightly brown), about 35 to 40 minutes.

STEP THREE: Cool in the pan to room temperature (or as soon as you are able to handle them) and transfer to a blender or the bowl of a food processor.

STEP FOUR: Make the dressing. Add ¹/₂ cup of the same vinegar you used when roasting the tomatoes and a tablespoon of honey to the tomatoes. (Since you can never be sure of the acidity content of the tomatoes, the sweetness of the honey will help stabilize the flavor.) Purée, drizzling in about 1¹/₂ cups of a neutral-tasting oil, like grapeseed or canola (neutral oil helps the tomato flavor shine through), until you achieve the thickness you prefer. Most people stop when their vinaigrette resembles melted ice cream; if yours is too thick, add a little warm water. Transfer to a jar and store in the fridge for up to 2 weeks.

MORE CHEF'S SECRETS . . .

FM: Do you have a favorite painting that features food?
DM: It's more of a "kitchen" painting—*Pink Cyclamen* by William B. Hoyt.

FM: Do you have a secret talent?
DM: Sculptor; my mother is an artist.

FM: What's your fantasy career?
DM: Landscape designer because I love gardening.

Steve SMITH

★ ★ ★ ★ ★ ★ ★

PROFILE

Steve Smith, who founded the first natural foods store and herb shop in Portland, Oregon, has spent more than thirty years immersed in the business of tea. In 1972, Smith, along with two partners, started Stash Tea Company, introducing herbal and specialty black teas to food service accounts, and it grew to become the second largest selling food-service tea in the country. When Stash Tea was sold in 1993, Smith looked to develop a product that would stimulate the industry, believing that consumers would welcome higher-quality and more interesting teas. Tazo was born, blending his talent for developing flavorful teas with his entrepreneurial spirit. Smith also was a founding member of the Herbal Tea Association in 1974; this group was instrumental in raising awareness for herbal products and setting standards still in use today.

HOW TO MAKE A PERFECT CUP OF TEA

★ ★ ★ ★ ★ ★ ★ ★ ★ ★ ★

The first important step in creating a good cup of tea is to use good-quality tea, and you should also give as much thought to the water. If the water isn't good enough to drink, it isn't good enough for making tea. Use filtered water instead.

STEP ONE: Do the math. The trickiest thing about using full-leaf tea is figuring out how much to use. (If you are brewing tea with a teabag, some of this work has already been done for you.) The recommended amount is approximately 1 teaspoon of tea per cup of water. Figure on 6 fluid ounces per "cup" of tea. If you're brewing tea in a large mug, which typically holds roughly 2 "cups," or 12 ounces, of water, use 2 teaspoons of full-leaf tea. If you're making a pot of tea, take the time before you brew to measure how much water it holds.

STEP TWO: Combine the tea with rapidly boiling water. Always start with cold filtered water, as water that has flowed through heaters and other dispensers is typically stale and a bit flat. "Rolling boil" is the operative phrase for most tea. Once the water is heated, preheat the pot or cup—add hot water and swirl it around and then discard. A cold pot or cup will rob the tea leaves of the heat they need to release their flavor and aroma. Next, add the appropriate amount of tea (see step one), pour water over the tea leaves, and cover the pot or mug to begin the steeping process.

STEP THREE: Determine the appropriate amount of steeping time. If the biggest threat to coffee quality is an unwillingness to use enough coffee, the corollary in tea is not allowing enough steeping time, resulting in weak tea. Some in the tea industry believe that the average person using a teabag allows only about 30 seconds of steeping time—enough time to get a bit of color into the cup, but not much character. As with other aspects of tea, the mix of traditions and cultures leads to a confusing array of methods and preferences for steeping time. Here are some general rules:

★ For green tea, allow about 3 minutes.
★ For oolong tea, allow 3 to 5 minutes.
★ For black tea, allow 5 minutes.
★ For herbal infusions, allow 5 minutes.

MORE CHEF'S SECRETS . . .

FM: Why does tea seem more romantic than coffee?
SS: Tea has a long history and has been important in cultures throughout the ages. The ritual and preparation of tea and the ceremony of tea, while a very personal experience, is one that can be shared with others.

FM: Do you have a favorite teacup or mug?
SS: I actually have two—one is a teacup and saucer from the Grand Hotel in Nuwara Eliya in Sri Lanka (a gift of the hotel staff), which is situated in the heart of one of the premier tea-growing regions. I love drinking tea from this cup, which I've had for about 5 years. The other is a *guywan*, which is a covered cup from China perfect for my current favorite Tazo tea, China Green Tips.

FM: What goes best with tea: sweets or savories?
SS: Of course tea goes with both. I find more traditional black teas such as Awake, Earl Grey, and Citron complement sweets, while some of our green teas are perfect with more savory dishes—teas like Green Ginger and Om. Flavored herbal teas such as Passion, Wild Sweet Orange, and Honeybush are just plain good with anything.

TEA TIPS FROM STEVE SMITH

STORAGE

★ Keep loose tea in a tightly closed container away from heat, moisture, and direct sunlight.

★ Keep tea away from strong odors. For some reason, tea is frequently stored in the spice cabinet at home, which is probably the worst place for it, as the tea leaves absorb odors rather easily. Tea will also pick up odors from other tea; if you store China Green Tips leaf tea in the same container that had been used for Earl Grey, you're asking for trouble.

★ Full-leaf tea can last up to 2 years in tightly sealed containers. Tea does not go stale as quickly or with such horrendous results as coffee does, as tea leaves don't have oils to go rancid. While coffee develops an off, stale taste, tea just becomes flatter and duller, losing its brisk edge as it ages.

TEA BAGS

★ As a rule, you'll get better results if you place the teabag(s) in the mug or pot and pour the boiling water onto the teabags. This simply creates more agitation and gets hotter water on the tea faster than putting the bag into the water.

★ Squeezing the teabag upon completion of brewing is a matter of choice and aesthetics. It will probably add a bit of flavor and decrease dripping. The downside, of course, is that you have to squeeze a teabag.

MEASURING

★ Full-leaf tea comes in an amazing variety of shapes and sizes. With some teas, you'd almost need the balance and dexterity of a juggler to get the spoon to hold even one leaf. Other teas have a much smaller particle size, meaning that you'll end up with more weight in the teaspoon and hence stronger tea. As a result, you will need to fill the spoon fuller as the leaf size increases, using a more rounded tea-spoon with larger leaves. With small, finely cut leaves, a level teaspoon is an accurate measure.

TEMPERATURE

★ Black and oolong teas and herbal infusions brew best with water as close to a boil as possible. There's an old adage in tea that you should "bring the pot to the kettle, not the kettle to the pot." This simply helps ensure the hottest water possible when making tea.

★ For green tea, virtually every tea book recommends slightly cooler water. The suggested temperature is usually around 180°F. Practically speaking, the best way to approach green tea is to boil the water, then let it cool for 1 to 2 minutes. Hotter water extracts more flavor, and when boiling water is poured on green tea, it seems to bring out harsher flavor elements; slightly cooler water extracts the softer, sweet flavor of green tea.

Sandro GAMBA

HOW TO PRESERVE THE ESSENCE OF WHITE TRUFFLES

★ ★ ★ ★ ★ ★ ★ ★ ★ ★ ★

One of the most coveted and costly food items is fresh imported white truffles, available only at the end of the fall through the midwinter months. When choosing truffles, look for a firm texture and strong aroma. It is critical to keep white truffles away from humidity, and never freeze them. They should be eaten within days of purchase, but if attended to properly, their essence can be preserved and enjoyed for weeks to come.

STEP ONE: Lightly wipe or brush the truffle with a soft cloth (like an all-natural cotton diaper, free of chemicals and fragrance) to remove the excess moisture and soil.

STEP TWO: Place the truffles in a jar with uncooked rice, dried pasta, or raw eggs still in the shell. Cover tightly and refrigerate for a maximum of 1 to 2 weeks. Check the maturation of the truffles each day—they should remain pale white in appearance.

STEP THREE: At your discretion (and as the truffles begin to deteriorate), remove the truffles from the jar. Reserve the wonderfully perfumed rice, pasta, or eggs and use to add a nice subtle truffle flavor to any pasta or rice dish. You can scramble the eggs or make an omelet.

STEP FOUR: Serve the truffles. White truffles are considered a condiment/garnish and therefore should always be eaten raw, never cooked, and sliced, not chopped, to preserve their earthy, garlicky aroma and taste. It is very common to serve white truffles with rice, eggs, or pasta. To get a bit fancy, you can slice them on top of beef or fish carpaccio, serve atop a tartine, or use as a great complementary garnish to soups as well as baked or mashed potatoes.

MORE CHEF'S SECRETS . . .

FM: Food you hate?
SG: I hate a piece of salad on my plate as decoration.

FM: Your favorite Sunday dinner?
SG: My wife's cooking.

FM: How would you like to be remembered in the culinary world?
SG: As being a classy chef.

Brian STREETER

PROFILE

Brian Streeter's interest in food started at an early age, when his stepfather shared his knowledge and passion for cooking. At the age of fourteen, Streeter began working in restaurant kitchens, and after graduation from high school, he attended the New England Culinary Institute in Montpelier, Vermont. As resident chef for Cakebread Cellars in the Napa Valley since 1989, Streeter highlights the world-class wines by basing his menus and recipes on local ingredients. The result is flavorful and uncontrived cooking, allowing the wine and food to complement each other, rather than compete. Streeter is also a member of the Chef's Collaborative, a national organization that sends chefs to elementary schools to teach children about sustainable agriculture and the different cuisines of the world.

HOW TO MAKE GARLIC PASTE

★ ★ ★ ★ ★ ★ ★ ★ ★ ★ ★

Even though I wouldn't want to give up my food processor (primarily for its speed), for some tasks it won't mash things fine enough. If I'm not in a hurry, the act of mashing ingredients by hand slows me down so that I feel more connected to the process of transforming ingredients into a finished dish. For example, when I want garlic to be chopped fine enough to dissolve into a sauce or marinade, a food processor won't do the job as well as a mortar and pestle will. But if you don't have a mortar and pestle, here's how to make a fine garlic paste using only a chef's knife.

STEP ONE: Break up a head of garlic into separate cloves.

STEP TWO: With the side of a knife, lightly press down on each clove to break the skin so that is easier to peel.

STEP THREE: Smash the cloves. Maybe you've seen a TV chef smash a clove of garlic on a cutting board with the side of a knife. To do so, place the side of the knife squarely over the center of the garlic clove. With the heel of your hand, whack the side of the knife to flatten the garlic against the cutting board. Repeat with the remaining cloves.

STEP FOUR: Roughly chop the garlic. Lightly sprinkle it with coarse salt. The salt granules act as an abrasive (like sand) to help grind the garlic and pull the juices out as well.

STEP FIVE: Smooth it out. With one hand on the handle of the knife (angled slightly on the horizontal to the work surface), and the other lightly pressing down on the side of the blade to guide it, use the tip (narrow end) of the blade to repeatedly mash the garlic against the cutting board until you obtain a smooth paste (at right). Now it's ready to add to an aioli, a Caesar salad dressing, or any other recipe that calls for mashed garlic.

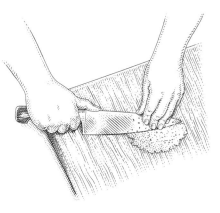

MORE CHEF'S SECRETS . . .

FM: What's your favorite kitchen tool?
BS: I was given a heavy stone mortar and pestle that now sits prominently on my counter.

FM: Do you have a food hero?
BS: My employers, Jack and Dolores Cakebread. They've given me one of the best chef's jobs in the Napa Valley.

FM: What's the biggest mistake people make when pairing food and wine?
BS: Not trusting their own tastes. Wine and food pairing is very subjective. There are no wrong answers. It's not supposed to be a test.

CHAPTER SEVEN

★ ★ ★ ★

DESSERTS & BAKING

Katrina MARKOFF

PROFILE

Katrina Markoff was born into a Macedonian family where food and family were the center of attention. One year she was given a Betty Crocker Easy-Bake oven for Christmas, and her destiny was sealed. In high school, she and her best friend, Julie, started a cake company, headquartered in their parents' kitchens. Although the business dissolved when the girls went to college, Markoff's interest did not. Three days after graduation from Vanderbilt University, she enrolled at Le Cordon Bleu in Paris. Fast-forward through the kitchens of Hotel Crillon in Paris as well as the fabled El Bulli in Rosas, Spain, and you end up at Vosges Haut-Chocolat, where Markoff specializes in exotic truffles. Headquartered in Chicago, the company has a second store located in New York's SoHo district.

HOW TO CHOP AND MELT CHOCOLATE

★ ★ ★ ★ ★ ★ ★ ★ ★ ★ ★ ★

The best desserts start with the best chocolate, generally available in an oversized bar or block. Since a block of chocolate can slip around when you are working, I chop mine with a five-prong ice chipper because it gives more control than a knife. Here are some tips for chopping, melting, and storing chocolate.

★ **To Chop:** Place the bar of chocolate on a clean, dry cutting board. Coming in at about a 50-degree angle, insert the ice pick firmly into the chocolate and sway your weight front and back until the chocolate breaks into a large shard. Continue until the chocolate is in pieces.

★ **To Measure:** Use a digital scale to weigh the amount of chocolate you need: That's the most accurate way.

★ **To Melt:** You can always melt chocolate in a double boiler over simmering (not boiling) water, but this can be tricky because condensation can cause moisture to get into the chocolate and make it "seize." If you want to be fast, you can easily melt chocolate in the microwave. Place chocolate in a plastic container and melt in 20-second intervals on medium power. Stir between intervals, as the microwave tends to pinpoint one area in the container—watch this area for burning. Even if the chocolate appears to be holding its exterior shape, the inside can be still be extremely hot.

★ **To Store:** Wrap any remaining chocolate tightly in plastic wrap and place in an airtight container. Chocolate tends to pick up other odors very quickly, so airflow is the enemy as far as storage goes. Stored properly at about 65°F, dark chocolate can last for 1 year, milk chocolate about 6 months, and white chocolate for 3 months.

MORE CHEF'S SECRETS . . .

FM: You specialize in truffles with unusual flavor combinations. What doesn't go with chocolate?
KM: Cumin.

FM: What is your favorite store-bought candy bar?
KM: Mars Bars—I love nougat and almond.

FM: They say that Paradise is a land of milk and honey. What is your idea of chocolate heaven?
KM: Dark chocolate waterfalls; white chocolate and wild huckleberry flowers that yield Rare White Volcano Island Honey pollen; milk chocolate mosaic walls in a slightly chilled room.

KATRINA MARKOFF'S FULL MOON BROWNIES

7 ounces Red Fire Bar (or bittersweet chocolate), in pieces
$^1/_2$ cup unsalted butter
3 tablespoons cocoa powder
3 large eggs
1 cup sugar
1 tablespoon vanilla extract
1 teaspoon salt
1 cup all-purpose flour

Preheat the oven to 350°F. Butter the bottom and sides of an 8-inch square baking pan and line with parchment paper. Then line with 2 pieces of aluminum foil perpendicular to each other (criss-crossing) so you can lift the brownies out of the pan with ease after baking.

Place the chocolate and butter in a medium-size, stainless steel bowl set over a pot of simmering water. Stir occasionally, until the chocolate has melted. Whisk in the cocoa powder until smooth; set aside.

In a mixing bowl, briefly whisk together the eggs, sugar, vanilla, and salt, about 30 seconds. Add the warm chocolate mixture; then mix in the flour just until combined. Do not overmix. Pour the batter into the prepared pan and bake for 35 minutes. The brownies will look shiny on the surface and slightly cracked on the top. Stick a toothpick into the brownies; the center should still be a bit gooey and sticky. Let the brownies cool for at least 1 hour before removing from the pan.

Wrap brownies in plastic and refrigerate for up to 5 days. Cut into squares to serve.

HOW TO TEMPER CHOCOLATE

★ ★ ★ ★ ★ ★ ★ ★ ★ ★ ★ ★ ★

Anyone can make chocolate candy at home—but you must first temper the chocolate. Tempering makes the chocolate easier to handle as a solid and gives a glossy appearance as well as a desirable "snap" to the candy when you bite into it. If you don't temper, chocolate can have a dull, matte appearance, develop spots, and be soft to the bite. This method works for all couverture, high-grade chocolate (though the temperature varies for milk chocolate—see step four).

STEP ONE: Break chocolate into chunks about ¹/₂ to ¹ inch across. Put the chocolate on a cutting board and use a strong, short-bladed knife or an ice pick. Insert the tip straight down into the chocolate until the chocolate cracks. Slicing chocolate does not work well.

STEP TWO: Melt chocolate in the top pan of a double boiler over water that is about 130°F. At Guittard, we are very much in favor of using thermometers. Use a rubber spatula in a gentle sweeping motion to stir the chocolate continually until about two-thirds of the chunks become liquid and about one-third are in soft lumps. Tumble the solid pieces around in the pan until they start to soften, gently lifting the chocolate off the bottom and sides to give it the greatest exposure to the warm surface of the pan. The temperature of the liquid chocolate at this point will be about 95°F.

Gary GUITTARD

PROFILE

The fourth-generation master chocolatier to run E. Guittard Chocolate Company, Gary Guittard was born and raised in San Francisco, where his great-grandfather opened the family business in 1868. After a boyhood spent working and eating his way around the factory, Guittard studied philosophy and film at the University of Denver before returning to help run his family's business. In 1988, he became the company's president and CEO and developed the E. Guittard artisan line by melding his knowledge of French chocolate-making with his family's nineteenth-century methods and recipes, even using a rare heirloom criollo cacao bean that was used in the 1930s.

STEP THREE: Remove the chocolate from the heat. Take the pan with the chocolate off the double boiler and use a kitchen towel to dry the bottom before placing it on the counter.

STEP FOUR: Continue stirring to cool the chocolate until the soft lumps disappear and the temperature lowers to 89°F (87°F for milk chocolate).

STEP FIVE: Test the chocolate. Check to see if the chocolate is ready and in good temper by placing a teaspoon of liquid chocolate on a scrap of parchment or waxed paper and placing it in the cooling area to set. A good cooling area would be in the breeze of an open window or door, or in a cool room, such as a basement, with a temperature of 60° to 70°F. The chocolate should begin to look dry on the surface in about 3 minutes. If this is so, begin with the dipping or molding. If not, continue stirring for another 3 minutes. As you test, leave the pot of chocolate suspended over the warm water, because the water will have also cooled to the correct temperature and will help to hold the chocolate temperature constant.

STEP SIX: If the chocolate starts to thicken, return the double boiler to the heat of the stovetop for about 30 seconds to reheat the water and soften the chocolate.

MORE CHEF'S SECRETS . . .

FM: It's your birthday. What's your dream dessert?
GG: A Dobosh torte with dark chocolate ganache frosting and chocolate cream between the soft, delectable layers.

FM: What was your favorite chocolate treat as a kid?
GG: Hot chocolate every morning and sometimes at night; also, chocolate nonpareils.

FM: How much chocolate do you eat in a typical workday?
GG: Three to six ounces; more if I miss lunch.

GARY GUITTARD'S TIPS FOR MAKING CHOCOLATE CANDY AT HOME

MOLDED CANDIES

★ Use a teaspoon or pastry bag to fill the molds with liquid chocolate. The chocolate will form a slight pyramid shape. After the mold is filled, gently tap it to level the chocolate.

DIPPED CANDIES

★ If the pieces being dipped have juice, salt, or crumbs coming off into the chocolate bath, it is best to first transfer a small amount of tempered chocolate into a smaller work bowl and dip from there to keep the whole tempered mass clean.

★ Have the fillings for the center of the candy ready on a baking tray.

★ Held on a fork, or with two fingers, an item can be swished through tempered chocolate. Then, by tapping the back of the fork or fingers against the rim of the bowl, the excess chocolate is encouraged to flow off of the piece.

★ Place the dipped pieces on an upside-down baking tray (for air circulation) that is covered with parchment or waxed paper.

François PAYARD

PROFILE

François Payard, a third-generation French pastry chef, honed his skills under his father and grandfather at his family's renowned shop, Au Nid des Friandises, on the Riviera before his talent earned him positions in several of France's finest kitchens: pastry chef in Paris at La Tour d'Argent as well as in the kitchen of Alan Senderens at Lucas Carton. His first New York job was as pastry chef at Le Bernardin, and he later joined Chef Daniel Boulud for the opening of Restaurant Daniel. Payard, a James Beard Pastry Chef of the Year, is the owner of Payard Patisserie & Bistro and the coauthor of *Simply Sensational Desserts: 140 Classics for the Home Baker from New York's Famous Patisserie and Bistro*.

HOW TO PIPE CHOCOLATE

★ ★ ★ ★ ★ ★ ★ ★ ★ ★ ★ ★

Home bakers often sacrifice putting that final, finished decorative touch on desserts because they think it is too difficult. But piping chocolate doesn't require a lot of skill—just some manual dexterity and a little bit of time.

STEP ONE: Make a cone out of an 8 x 12-inch rectangle of parchment paper.
- ★ Cut the rectangle in half diagonally.
- ★ Hold a triangle, with the right angle in the upper right corner, between the thumb and forefinger of your left hand, halfway down the hypotenuse.
- ★ With your right hand, bring the bottom point in on itself, curling the paper to make a cone (Figure A).
- ★ Holding the cone in your left hand, twist the tail around the cone (Figure B), pulling it to tighten. Tuck in the ends to secure (Figures C—D).

Chocolate becomes more difficult to pipe once it cools so it is a good idea to make a second cone and keep it warm in a low oven.

STEP TWO: Secure the cone by standing it up in a bowl of sugar or a short narrow glass and fill it about halfway with melted chocolate. If you have melted the chocolate in a double boiler, make sure that none of the condensation water drips into the cone.

STEP THREE: Seal the cone by folding over the open end, and snip off the tip to create the piping "tube." Be careful: If the hole is too large, the chocolate will run out too freely; too small, and you won't get the flow necessary to pipe.

STEP FOUR: Pipe the chocolate to make a decoration. To decorate a plated dessert (or write a name): Hold the back of the cone with your dominant hand so that your fingers can pinch the cone, squeezing out the chocolate, and use your other hand to direct the tip. To finish a line, stop squeezing the chocolate through the tip just before you come to the finishing point or, alternately, gently touch the tip to the surface just at the point you wish to stop.

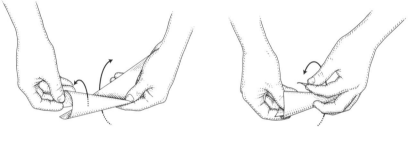

Figure A

Figure B

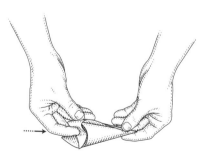

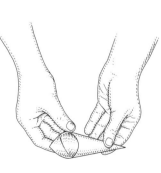

Figure C

Figure D

To make decorations ahead of time: Pipe melted chocolate onto the back of a warm baking sheet and refrigerate until set. Use a small offset spatula (with a flexible tongue) to remove the decorations and transfer them to dessert plates.

MORE CHEF'S SECRETS . . .

FM: Favorite over-the-counter candy bar?
FP: Kit Kat or Bounty.

FM: Best market in the world?
FP: Greenmarket at Union Square, New York City.

FM: Kitchen motto?
FP: Work clean and organized.

HOW TO MAKE THE BEST GANACHE EVER

★ ★ ★ ★ ★ ★ ★ ★ ★ ★ ★ ★

"Make the ganache!" "Cut the ganache!" These instructions were almost lost in the hum of the enrobing line at Bernachon, a famous chocolatier in Lyons, France. It was 1995, and I was a chocolate neophyte when Bernachon allowed me to spend 2 weeks in their small factory, where I learned much more than I helped. Before Bernachon, I literally had never heard the word *ganache*. It wasn't until several years later, when I tried making my own, that I came up with this method. Although the classic technique calls for hot cream poured over finely chopped chocolate, my method is to heat both the chocolate and the cream. Here's how I do it.

STEP ONE: Simultaneously heat the chocolate and the cream. Chop 8 ounces of the best bittersweet chocolate and melt it in the top of a double boiler or in a bowl suspended over a water bath. Heat 3/4 cup heavy cream in a heavy saucepan until it just begins to simmer.

STEP TWO: Allow both the chocolate and the cream to cool until it registers between 115° and 120°F on a chocolate thermometer or a digital meat thermometer.

STEP THREE: Slowly pour the chocolate into the cream, carefully whisking as you pour. This method treats the ganache like an oil and vinegar emulsion and keeps the mixture from separating.

Robert STEINBERG

★ ★ ★ ★ ★ ★ ★ ★ ★ ★

PROFILE

In 1994, Robert Steinberg, a physician and accomplished cook, got into a conversation about making chocolate with coffee roaster Bob Voorhees, who thought Steinberg's background in both food and science would be a perfect fit for the craft. In search of a chocolate education, Steinberg worked at Bernachon, a small family-owned chocolate maker in Lyon, France, and soon began to think seriously about making chocolate in the United States. In early 1996, he and former patient John Scharffenberger, a California winemaker, founded Scharffen Berger Chocolate Maker, using artisanal European production methods. Scharffen Berger chocolate, the choice of some of the country's finest dessert makers, is available nationally. Steinberg continues to practice medicine at the San Francisco Free Clinic.

The ganache should ultimately be smooth and shiny. While warm, it can be used as icing. If allowed to cool (either at room temperature or in the refrigerator) to the consistency of thick peanut butter, the ganache makes luscious centers for truffles.

MORE CHEF'S SECRETS . . .

FM: You're a doctor and a chocolatier. What other career combinations would you consider?
RS: Write, live, and work in another country (France comes to mind since I have friends there); act (I studied acting in New York in the early eighties and considered pursuing it seriously); and build a house.

FM: What's your favorite indulgence food?
RS: Pasta, pickled herring, half-sour pickles, *natto* (fermented soybeans).

FM: Do you have a culinary muse?
RS: I remember watching Julia Child on black-and-white television about 40 years ago and still admire her intelligence and independence. I also love the way Elizabeth David, A. J. Liebling, and Calvin Trillin write about food.

HOW TO MAKE A CHOCOLATE SOUFFLÉ DAYS IN ADVANCE

★ ★ ★ ★ ★ ★ ★ ★ ★ ★ ★ ★

Soufflés are among the most intimidating desserts to make. A typical soufflé is made by mixing up a base (restaurants usually use a flavored pastry cream), folding in egg whites, and immediately baking at a high temperature. Usually, you must serve the dessert right away because it falls quickly. But this soufflé is magical, because the technique allows the chocolate to "sit up" and hold in the air—meaning you can mix it days in advance, then pop it in the oven when you want it.

STEP ONE: Prepare the ramekins. Melt butter and brush evenly into ten to twelve 6-ounce ramekins. Coat the insides of the ramekins with granulated sugar, making sure you cover the sides and bottom entirely. This is very important because the soufflé needs to rise evenly, and the sugar coating prevents the mixture from sticking to the sides of the ramekin when it bakes.

STEP TWO: Melt 8 ounces of couverture chocolate in a double boiler over hot water. Couverture chocolate is a special variety used for candymaking. It has more cocoa butter than regular chocolate; the best has at least 55 percent cacao.

STEP THREE: Combine 2 cups of egg whites (from about 10 jumbo eggs) and 1¼ cups granulated sugar and whip to stiff peaks in a mixer.

Jason FOSS

· · · · · · · ·

PROFILE

Originally from South Dakota, Jason Foss grew up working in the kitchen at his parents' steakhouse. Destined for a career in the culinary arts, Foss graduated from the Bakery and Pastry Program at the Culinary Institute of America and honed his European pastry skills with Jean-Claude Canestrier at the Paris Casino in Las Vegas. Foss then met fellow CIA graduate Douglas Brown and accompanied him to the James Beard House in New York City as pastry chef. The duo teamed up again at the Landmark Restaurant at the Melrose Hotel in Dallas, where Foss was named Best Pastry Chef by *D* magazine.

STEP FOUR: Beat the melted chocolate into the whites with the mixer on high. Mix until incorporated completely (no white streaks).

STEP FIVE: Pipe the mixture from a pastry bag or spoon it into the prepared ramekins. Level the tops so they are even, cover, and refrigerate immediately. The mix can be refrigerated for 4 or 5 days.

STEP SIX: When you're ready to bake them, place the soufflés in a 425°F oven for 15 to 20 minutes. They will rise 2 to 3 inches above the edge of the ramekins. Serve immediately with your desired sauce.

MORE CHEF'S SECRETS . . .

FM: It's your birthday—what's for breakfast?
JF: Since my birthday is December 24, a very busy day at the hotel, my answer is probably not what you'd expect—Mountain Dew and doughnuts.

FM: Lunch?
JF: More Mountain Dew or coffee.

FM: Dinner?
JF: A glass of red wine and osso bucco with fresh pasta.

HOW TO MAKE A CHOCOLATE BAG

★ ★ ★ ★ ★ ★ ★ ★ ★ ★ ★ ★

I was asked to cook a dinner for a group of six-teen executive chefs coming to town. My thought was that since these guys create "frou-frou" food all day long for a living, I wanted to have fun and take the seriousness out of the whole dinner. The meal was whimsical, and I wanted to end with a simple milk chocolate mousse served in a funky way—the grocery bag idea popped in my mind and a coffee bag was handy. The rest is history. Here's how I did it.

STEP ONE: Acquire 6 to 8 small coffee-bean bags. Your local grocery store usually is amenable to selling (or giving) you several small coffee bean bags. These bags are a must for this trick—they are lined with a plastic coating that is perfect for "painting" on the melted chocolate.

STEP TWO: Cut the coffee bags off to a height of about 3 inches. Then cut out a little inverted 1/2-inch half-circle in the middle of the top of the bag to imitate the look of a paper grocery bag.

STEP THREE: Melt 4 cups of semisweet chocolate morsels in a double boiler over low heat. Chocolate chips, available in any grocery store, make stronger bags than fine Belgian or French chocolate.

**STEP FOUR: Using a small pastry brush, "paint" the melted chocolate over the interior of the

Lisa DUPAR

★ ★ ★ ★ ★ ★ ★ ★

PROFILE
Lisa Dupar's culinary skills took root on the beach in South Carolina, where she spent her days shrimping and her evenings helping to prepare family meals. In 1976, Dupar moved to Atlanta and spent 3 years studying in the culinary program of the Westin Peachtree Plaza Hotel. After graduation, Dupar moved to Zurich as the lead evening chef in the dining room of Baron du Moulette, and then to Geneva, where she worked creating fine chocolates and pastries for Hôtel de la Paix and the Hôtel du Rhône. Returning to the States, Dupar became the first female chef for Westin International at the Palm Court Restaurant in the Seattle Westin Hotel. In 1986, she opened Lisa Dupar Catering, establishing her reputation in the Puget Sound region for refined serv-ice and fresh creations.

bag, starting at the bottom and working your way up the sides to the top. Be generous with the volume of chocolate that you paint on. If it is too thin, it will crack when you peel the paper bag off and you will lose the whole thing. After the insides of the bags are thoroughly coated with chocolate, gently stand them upright on a cookie sheet.

STEP FIVE: Refrigerate the bags until the chocolate is completely chilled, about 30 minutes. You can also store the bags in the refrigerator, unpeeled, until you need them.

STEP SIX: Gently peel away the bag at a corner; then snip the paper off a little at a time with scissors. Continue peeling and snipping until all the paper is off.

STEP SEVEN: Serve. The bags are fairly sturdy at this point and can hold mousse or Bavarian cream for a plated dessert. I have also filled them with candies and wrapped them in cellophane to give to the kids on Halloween.

MORE CHEF'S SECRETS . . .

FM: It's your birthday. What's for dinner?
LD: It's in the summer, so heirloom tomatoes with basil and mozzarella. I'll also be sipping a 2002 Marenco Brachetto d'Acqui into the evening with friends.

FM: What's your favorite kitchen appliance?
LD: My Viking range.

FM: What was the silliest food trend?
LD: Jell-O shots—if you consider that a food or a trend. What a way to ruin good Jell-O and good vodka.

Michael LAISKONIS

PROFILE

Initially educated in the visual arts, Michael Laiskonis trained in a number of Detroit pastry shops and worked as both sous chef and pastry chef at Emily's in Northville, Michigan, before becoming pastry chef at Tribute, one of *Gourmet* magazine's America's Best Restaurants, under executive chef Takashi Yagihashi. He has been twice named one of the 10 Best Pastry Chefs in America by *Pastry Art & Design*. Laiskonis's training and work experience—divided between pastry and savory realms—are a primary influence in his culinary approach.

HOW TO SPRAY-PAINT WITH CHOCOLATE

★ ★ ★ ★ ★ ★ ★ ★ ★ ★ ★ ★

With every trip to the hardware store, I find one more item that might have an application in pastry work. Sure, there are products to be found through the typical channels of pastry suppliers, but the same item at a hardware store may be less expensive or more durable. I tend to wander the hardware store aisles with thoughts of ganache rather than garden hoses, and I am obsessed with Home Depot.

Haunting the hardware store is by no means a new idea, at least among savvy pastry chefs. Chocolate is notorious for being a rather fickle product to work with. But with the technical know-how and a touch of ingenuity, we've come to create some pretty amazing things. How might we elegantly coat the surface of, say, a mousse, tart, or cake with chocolate? With what tools can we preserve taste, texture, and appearance? Why not a paint sprayer? Yes, an electric paint sprayer (with refillable plastic canister). Two caveats: Always thoroughly clean a brand-new sprayer before running chocolate through it, and never use the same apparatus as intended—to spray actual paint!

STEP ONE: Choose a paint sprayer that fits your grip and is light enough to handle comfortably.

STEP TWO: Thin the chocolate by combining it with cocoa butter. While melted chocolate can be quite fluid, it is usually too thick to travel the inner labyrinth of the paint sprayer. Pastry chefs usually thin out their spraying chocolate by melting cocoa butter with it, typically in proportions of 50 percent chocolate and 50 percent cocoa butter. Once this mixture is completely melted and smooth, you're ready for action. From this basic recipe, you can further branch out to create different tones, from dark to milk chocolate and even white chocolate.

STEP THREE: Spray the chocolate on a chilled dessert plate. The most amazing quality of sprayed chocolate is its velvet-like appearance. Whether you are decorating a plate or an individual dome or disk of mousse, that stunning effect can only be produced with a sprayer. To best achieve this, anything you spray must be chilled so that the tiny droplets of airborne chocolate adhere and instantly solidify, creating the "velvet." And because the sum total of chocolate coating the item is rather small (it will instantly melt at the touch or in the mouth), you can maintain delicacy and elegance, and even flavor.

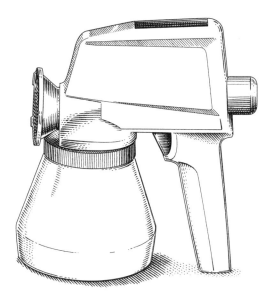

MORE CHEF'S SECRETS . . .

FM: Favorite indulgence food?
ML: When you spend an entire day analyzing food, sometimes you have to find comfort in the polar opposite of haute cuisine. I confess that, after a long shift, sometimes the only thing that works is a frozen pizza!

FM: Top kitchen priority?
ML: In the professional kitchen, my staff of assistants is my greatest tool and asset. I can't do it all myself! In an overall sense, however, cleanliness and organization are paramount, as is timing.

FM: Best Sunday dinner?
ML: I try to take Sunday off, both physically and mentally (come Monday, my other night off, however, I'm in charge of cooking dinner). My wife and I have a long-standing Sunday ritual—an afternoon movie and takeout from our favorite Thai "hole-in-the-wall." For special occasions and holidays, I only need utter a few words—Italian mother-in-law.

HOW TO IMPART VANILLA FLAVOR

★ ★ ★ ★ ★ ★ ★ ★ ★ ★ ★ ★ ★

To a pastry chef, a vanilla bean is like salt—the addition of it to any dessert recipe instantly enhances the flavor. One of the simplest ways to infuse vanilla flavor into a dessert is by substituting homemade vanilla sugar for granulated sugar whenever it is called for in a recipe. Here's how I do it.

STEP ONE: Slice a whole vanilla bean in half and scrape out the seeds with a knife. Reserve the seeds for another use.

STEP TWO: Place the vanilla bean halves on a sheet pan and dry in a preheated 200°F oven until crisp, about 45 minutes.

STEP THREE: Transfer the dried vanilla bean halves to a food processor. Add 1/4 cup of granulated sugar. Pulse until fine in consistency—the sugar helps to grind the beans down to the right consistency.

STEP FOUR: Pass the vanilla sugar through a *tamis* (a drum-shaped sieve) into a mixing bowl. Discard the contents of the *tamis*.

STEP FIVE: Add another cup of sugar to the bowl. Store in an airtight container and use in almost any baking recipe that calls for sugar.

Tracy Kamperdyk ASSUE

★ ★ ★ ★ ★ ★ ★ ★ ★ ★ ★ ★ ★

PROFILE

A graduate of the Culinary Institute of America, Tracy Kamperdyk Assue began her cooking career in some of New York City's finest restaurants before finding her specialty: the pastry department. After working as an assistant pastry chef with David Burke at the River Café and at Lespinasse with Richard Leach and Gray Kunz, Assue is now executive pastry chef at three City Limits Diner locations (two in White Plains, New York, and one in Stamford, Connecticut, all owned by longtime New York restaurateur John Livanos), where she prepares everything from scratch, including artisanal breads as well as a full range of pies, tarts, cakes, and her signature granola.

MORE CHEF'S SECRETS . . .

FM: What was your favorite childhood dessert?
TKA: My Aunt Grace's twists; I remember them being so buttery, warm, and incredibly comforting.

FM: What's the first thing you think children should learn to bake?
TKA: Cookies, because they are simple to make and children love eating them.

FM: How tall can a dessert be before it topples over?
TKA: It's all relative. With enough time and patience, anything is possible.

HOW TO KEEP COOKIE DOUGH HANDY

★ ★ ★ ★ ★ ★ ★ ★ ★ ★ ★ ★

As a child, I watched my mother roll pie dough between two sheets of waxed paper to prevent the dough from sticking to the counter and make it easier to transfer to a pie plate. Years later, I was testing a delicate shortbread dough and no matter how hard I tried, I couldn't roll it out without using a good amount of flour, which toughened the fragile dough. I remembered my mother's trick and it worked beautifully. I took it one step further with advice from my baker friend Amanda Gamble and began storing well-wrapped rolled dough in the refrigerator or freezer. It is always at my fingertips, ready to bake whenever the occasion arises. Here's how you can do the same.

STEP ONE: Place a piece of cooking parchment or waxed paper on the counter, with the side that curls facing the countertop so the paper lies relatively flat.

STEP TWO: Roughly judge the amount of dough your paper can accommodate and scoop the dough out into the center of the paper. If you put down too much dough, you can always scrape or cut away the excess.

STEP THREE: Flatten the dough slightly and put another piece of paper on top, pressing the dough out as far as possible with your hands.

Maria Helm SINSKEY

★ ★ ★ ★ ★ ★ ★

PROFILE

Maria Helm Sinskey entered the world of professional kitchens at age sixteen when she took an after-school cooking job. Enrolling in Union College, she temporarily satisfied her strong culinary desire when she became her sorority house chef. After graduation, Sinskey attended the California Culinary Academy and worked in several Bay Area restaurants. As executive chef of PlumpJack Café, she was selected as one of *Food & Wine* magazine's Best New Chefs. Now married to vintner Robert Sinskey and mother of two, Sinskey is the culinary director of food and wine programs at Robert Sinskey Vineyards in Napa and the author of *The Vineyard Kitchen*, a book of seasonal menus paired with just the right wines.

STEP FOUR: Roll the dough out to the thickness you desire.

STEP FIVE: Slide the rolled dough (still encased in its paper) onto a sheet pan and transfer to your refrigerator or freezer.

STEP SIX: After the dough is chilled and rigid, wrap it tightly (and quickly) in plastic wrap. Well-wrapped cookie dough can be stored in the freezer for up to 3 months. It is not necessary to wrap dough that will be used within the day.

STEP SEVEN: To use the dough, remove it from the refrigerator or freezer. Peel off the top sheet of paper. If you used parchment, use the top sheet to line your cookie sheet. Frozen cookie dough should be thawed for a few minutes to avoid cracking when it is cut. Refrigerated dough can be cut immediately.

MORE CHEF'S SECRETS . . .

FM: What's the best culinary gift you ever received?
MHS: A basket of beautiful morels and an amazingly pungent summer truffle from Connie Green, our local mushroom forager, just when I needed them.

FM: Who has had the biggest impact on your cooking style?
MHS: My great-grandmother Nana DiGregorio, my grandmothers, Antoinette Baker and Gertrude Helm, and my mother and father, Bob and Barbara Helm.

FM: What's your idea of a perfect Sunday dinner?
MHS: An omelet with fresh herbs, a little green salad, and a chilled glass of Beaujolais or other fruity red wine.

HOW TO MAKE PERFECT PIE CRUST

★ ★ ★ ★ ★ ★ ★ ★ ★ ★ ★ ★

Shelley YOUNG

★ ★ ★ ★ ★ ★ ★ ★ ★ ★

Pie has a unique place in our social system. When you arrive at a party bearing a homemade apple pie, you will instantaneously be added to every party guest list in town. Sadly though, a good pie seems to be a thing of the past. Here are some pie-making tips that are sure to get you on everyone's invitation list.

STEP ONE: Choose a proper pie pan. A pie should have a light, flaky, golden brown crust, and that starts with pie pans made from material that conducts heat well (like ceramic, porcelain, and cast iron). The right pie pan ensures even heat distribution, resulting in a crunchier bottom crust, and heat retention, so that when you open and close the oven to check on the pie's progress, the pan will stay hot. Since the crust is in direct contact with the dish, fluctuations in the temperature of the pie dish will slow down the cooking of the crust while the filling retains its heat and continues to cook—resulting in an undercooked crust and an overcooked filling.

STEP TWO: Chill your dough thoroughly. Chill your dough well by dividing it in half, shaping each piece into a nicely formed disk, and wrapping it in plastic wrap. Although most recipes tell you to chill your pastry dough for 2 hours, it is better to chill it for at least 8 hours, or even overnight. This is true for a variety of reasons, including:

PROFILE

Shelley Young grew up in a small town in Iowa where her parents owned the local antique shop. Her prototypical wholesome midwestern upbringing included childhood summers spent putting up beans, corn, and tomatoes and pitting sour cherries for homemade pies. After earning a culinary degree from Des Moines Area Community College, Young moved to Southern California, where she was the chef at Charlie's Grill in San Diego. Deciding to move back east, Young chose Chicago as the site for her newest venture, the Chopping Block, a cookware shop and cooking school in Lincoln Park.

★ **Consistency:** If you chill it for just 2 hours, the dough is cold on the outside but not yet on the inside, so when you roll it, you roll two different consistencies. The chilled outside edge tends to be crumbly and crack, while the center is warm and sticky.

★ **Stickiness:** Ideally, a well-chilled crust is drier and less sticky, requiring less flour on the board when rolling out the dough. The less flour you use when rolling, the better, as this makes for a more tender crust.

STEP THREE: Remove the dough from the refrigerator as needed. After your dough is well chilled, take each disk out of the refrigerator as you need it. If you are making a one-crust pie, put the extra disk of dough in a ziplock bag and freeze it. (It can keep for up to 6 months; remove it from the freezer and thaw in the refrigerator for 24 hours when needed.) Keep the dough as cold as possible while you are working with it.

STEP FOUR: Soften the dough. I flatten the dough slightly by smacking it with a rolling pin about 10 times, which seems to soften it just enough to make it workable.

STEP FIVE: Lightly flour your work surface and start rolling. I flip the dough (as many times as the dough will allow it without ripping) and spread a new, light layer of flour under it so the dough doesn't stick to the counter. (I do this each time I flip the dough.) I like to use a wooden surface to roll crusts since its texture tends to grab the dough and keep it from slipping while I'm rolling.

STEP SIX: Settle the rolled dough into the pie dish. After you've rolled the dough into a circle, place your rolling pin in the center of the dough and wrap the dough over the pin; then lift it into the pie pan. Gently push the dough into the pan and fold the extra dough underneath the edges. Crimp the edge or press a fork around the edge to create a decorative border.

STEP SEVEN: Chill the dough again. I suggest chilling your pie dough again at this point if you are making a one-crust pie. This extra step means colder butter and shortening in the dough, which melt more slowly and thus create a flakier crust. The colder the dough is when it goes in the oven, the flakier the crust will be!

MORE CHEF'S SECRETS . . .

FM: Favorite cookbook?

SY: It's really a toss-up between *Sundays at Moosewood Restaurant* by the Moosewood Collective and *Cookwise* by Shirley Corriher. *Sundays* is one of the best collections of well-tested recipes I've ever seen. Shirley's ability to demystify the science of cooking has brought a new level of understanding to the every-day cook.

FM: First thing anyone should learn to make?

SY: Cookies are a great place to start. Most people like them, they are easy to prepare, and they demonstrate a large quantity of sweet and savory cooking techniques.

FM: Fancy recipe worth mastering?

SY: Pâté and terrines. With the invention of the food processor, they are incredibly easy to prepare.

Tamasin
DAY LEWIS

★ ★ ★ ★ ★ ★ ★

PROFILE

Tamasin Day Lewis, one of the first women to be accepted by King's College, Cambridge, is a writer, producer, and director of films and documentaries for British television, including *British Rites*, winner of the Royal Television Society Award/Social Education. Day Lewis, who currently writes a food column for the Saturday edition of the *Daily Telegraph*, is also the author of *West of Ireland Summers*, *Simply the Best: The Art of Seasonal Cooking*, *The Art of the Tart: Savory and Sweet*, and *Tarts with Tops On: Or How to Make the Perfect Pie*.

HOW TO BAKE A BLIND PIE CRUST

★ ★ ★ ★ ★ ★ ★ ★ ★ ★ ★ ★

You should only bake a blind (empty) pie crust when a recipe calls for it. This is usually the case for sweet fruit tarts, which rely on the pastry being cooked without the filling because they are frequently filled with a crème patisserie and then decorated with fresh fruit.

STEP ONE: Preheat the oven to about 375°F. Allow the unbaked dough to chill inside the fridge for at least 30 minutes, or refrigerate it overnight.

STEP TWO: Line a greased pie pan with dough. Never stretch it to fit; it will stretch back. Tear off a piece of wax paper slightly larger than the pie pan and place it over the dough. Cover the paper with a layer of dried beans to prevent the pie crust from rising up in the oven.

STEP THREE: When the dough is nearly cooked (the timing will depend on the recipe you are using), take the pie pan out of the oven, remove the paper and the beans, and prick the bottom of the pie shell with a fork to let out trapped air that would otherwise bubble up.

STEP FOUR: Brush the partly baked pie shell with a light coating of beaten egg or egg white to ensure a crisp finished tart. Return the pie pan to the oven, and continue baking for another 5 to 10 minutes to dry the bottom of the tart.

MORE CHEF'S SECRETS . . .

FM: Favorite food store?
TDL: Murray's Cheese Shop on Bleecker Street in New York City, because I am a passionate advocate of raw milk cheeses, and the owner sources his cheese from small dairies.

FM: Favorite book about food (not a cookbook)?
TDL: *Honey from a Weed* by Patience Gray.

FM: Favorite food scene in a movie?
TDL: *La Grande Bouffe*—obscenely, pornographically, lushly greedy from start to finish.

Emile CASTILLO

HOW TO PERFECT CRÈME CARAMEL

★ ★ ★ ★ ★ ★ ★ ★ ★ ★ ★ ★

Often while eating a crème caramel, you will see a lot of tiny holes made by air bubbles that form during baking. A well-cooked crème caramel should have a smooth and dense texture, and I know just the way to achieve that.

STEP ONE: Place the crème caramel cups in a roasting pan with a protective layer between the pan and the cups. When your favorite recipe for crème caramel is ready for baking (I suggest the recipe on pages 198–199), cover the bottom of a roasting pan with old newspaper or a piece of cardboard and place the crème caramel cups on top. This even protective layer will prevent the molds from having direct contact with the heat, keeping the mixture from reaching a boil. (When the mixture boils, bubbles form.)

STEP TWO: Add water to the roasting pan. Add enough hot water to the roasting pan to rise about halfway up the sides of the molds.

STEP THREE: Place the pan on the stove and bring the water to a simmer.

STEP FOUR: Bake. Place the pan in a preheated 350°F oven and bake the crème caramel for 40 to 50 minutes.

STEP FIVE: Check for doneness. To make sure that the crème caramel is cooked, insert the blade of a knife (make sure the knife is completely dry) into the center of the cup. The knife blade should come out clean and feel slightly warm to the touch.

MORE CHEF'S SECRETS . . .

FM: What is your favorite time of day to eat breakfast?
EC: My favorite time to eat breakfast is at seven in the morning. But at Norma's, we eat breakfast all day, every day!

FM: What is the first thing you do when you enter the kitchen?
EC: The first thing that I do when entering the kitchen is to make my rounds through all the kitchen areas and greet everyone.

FM: What is the last thing you do before you leave?
EC: I make another round through the kitchen and wish everyone a pleasant evening.

EMILE CASTILLO'S RECIPE
FOR CRÈME CARAMEL

1 quart milk
1 vanilla bean, cut in half lengthwise
6 whole eggs
2 egg yolks
$2/3$ cup sugar, plus 1 cup
$1/2$ cup water
6 to 8 crème caramel molds or ramekins

Preheat the oven to 350°F.

In a saucepan, combine the milk with the vanilla bean, bringing the milk to a boil. Remove from heat; set aside and allow to cool for 10 minutes. Discard the vanilla bean.

In a mixing bowl, whisk together the eggs, egg yolks, and $2/3$ cup of sugar. When the sugar has dissolved, add the milk in small quantities while continuing to whisk.

In a heavy-bottomed, nonreactive saucepan, combine the remaining 1 cup sugar and the water to make the caramel. Bring the mixture to a boil while stirring carefully and continue to cook until the mixture becomes golden brown. When you have a nice golden caramel, place the bottom of the saucepan in a bowl of cold water to stop the cooking process. (In order to get the right color, this has to happen very quickly. The sugar keeps on cooking and continues to darken.) While the caramel is still warm (quickly, before it hardens), pour a small amount into each crème caramel mold to form a thin layer on the bottom.

Cover the bottom of a roasting pan with some folded newspaper or cardboard. Arrange the molds in the pan and fill them three-quarters full with the crème caramel mixture. Add enough hot water to the pan to come halfway up the sides of the molds. Place the pan on the stove and bring the water to a simmer.

Bake at 350°F for 45 to 50 minutes. When the custard is fully cooked, remove the pan from the oven. Allow the molds to cool at room temperature in the pan; then remove and refrigerate until ready to serve.

To unmold the crème caramel, run a knife around the rim of the mold to loosen the custard. Invert the mold over a dessert plate and carefully shake the custard out. Garnish with whipped cream, caramel sauce, or fresh berries.

Nick TISCHLER

HOW TO SHAPE ICE CREAM

★ ★ ★ ★ ★ ★ ★ ★ ★ ★ ★ ★

I think I've been carrying this idea since my childhood because we were a family of big ice cream eaters, especially Carvel ice cream cakes. Then, one day at Snackbar, where time constraints mean that I functionally need to stop scooping ice cream, it just popped into my head.

STEP ONE: Line a simply structured mold with clear plastic wrap and set aside. Ornate shapes will not release the ice cream as well, so I recommend using a rectangle or ring. It also helps to choose a mold made from lightweight material, like metal or plastic, because the full mold will be lighter and easier to handle.

STEP TWO: Unmold the ice cream from the container. Cut it into small pieces, and place the pieces in a mixing bowl. Using the back of a wooden spoon, mash the pieces together until you have soft, smooth (but not melted) ice cream.

STEP THREE: Using a soft rubber spatula, pack the mold with ice cream. The ice cream should pack densely, without air bubbles. Give the mold a few whacks by dropping it on the counter several times so that the ice cream will settle and you will get rid of remaining air bubbles.

STEP FOUR: Place the uncovered mold in the freezer. Don't try to cover the mold yet—plastic wrap will stick to the softened ice cream.

STEP FIVE: When the ice cream is slightly set (about 6 hours), cover it with clear plastic wrap and return to the freezer until firm (about another 8 hours).

STEP SIX: Remove the mold from the freezer, uncover, and invert over a serving platter or plastic cutting board. If the ice cream doesn't release, rub a hot, wet towel over the exterior of the mold (but don't wet the ice cream) to help release the ice cream all in one piece.

STEP SEVEN: Immediately slice the ice cream into serving pieces (just like a cake), or cut each slice in half diagonally, making decorative triangles to serve with tuiles, biscotti, or any other crisp cookie.

MORE CHEF'S SECRETS . . .

FM: You were the executive chef with NBC for the 2002 Olympics in Deer Valley, Utah. What was your gold medal event?
NT: Fish cookery. I rose through the ranks as *poissonnier* at New York's top restaurants—Aquavit, Lutèce, Aureole, and Bouley. I've been told that I can do no wrong with delicacies from the sea; I make a point to keep each fish at the texture that it should be.

FM: Name an unsung food hero.
NT: Chef Boyardee. He is an amazing chef. I can swallow a whole can of beef ravioli.

FM: What's your favorite private moment snack?
NT: Ring Dings. Lots of them.

CHAPTER EIGHT

★ ★ ★ ★

EQUIPMENT

Norman KORNBLEUTH

HOW TO SELECT A CHEF'S KNIFE

★ ★ ★ ★ ★ ★ ★ ★ ★ ★ ★ ★ ★

Selecting a knife is a personal, intimate act. What makes a knife right for you is not just the size of the blade, it's the heft of the knife—how it feels in your hand. Although there is a wide range of knives available, an excellent starting point in building a collection is a multipurpose (or chef's) knife with a high-carbon stainless steel blade; it is easy to sharpen, holds its edge, and doesn't rust. Choose a knife using the following guidelines.

★ **Start by picking a knife that reflects the amount you're able to pay.** You can go up or down in cost (and quality) from there.

★ **Check the knife for comfort.** Pay special attention to the shape of the bolster (where the handle meets the blade). Some bolsters are squareish, while others are contoured. The contoured bolsters are usually more comfortable.

★ **Check the knife's balance.** Grab the knife in a claw-like grip with your fingers sharing both the blade and the handle. This is the balance point—holding it here will give you the most control.

★ **Note the length of the blade.** The length of the blade ranges from 6 to 12 inches, and its length affects the way the knife rocks in your hand. Smaller, thinner blades are more manageable, but the longer your blade the more you can chop at one time.

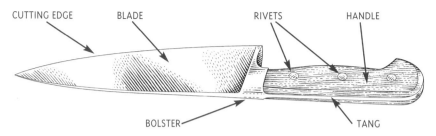

CUTTING EDGE   BLADE   RIVETS   HANDLE

BOLSTER   TANG

★ **Check out the heft—whether the knife is too heavy or too light in your hand.** You should be able to count on the weight of the knife and the force of gravity to make your tasks easier.

★ **Observe the knife as a whole; the cutting edge is not always what sets the price.** Note the finish and workmanship by looking down at the tang (the extension of the metal through the handle) and check it for smoothness. Also make sure there are no cracks or crevices (where debris can collect) near the rivets.

MORE CHEF'S SECRETS . . .

FM: What is your favorite culinary (tool) gift?
NK: The Lever Model Screwpull wine opener because it is beautifully designed and easy to use. Although it has been endlessly copied, this is the original, and I love the look of it.

FM: What do you consider to be an essential kitchen utensil?
NK: In addition to a multipurpose or chef's knife, I need locking tongs (with a sliding bar lock for easy storage) for turning steaks on the grill, and a chinois for straining and sieving sauces and soups. Once you get one, you won't know how you lived without it.

FM: Name the most overrated specialty appliance.
NK: There are so many, from the bread machine to the George Foreman Grill.

Andrew SUTTON

PROFILE

Texas native Andrew Sutton, a graduate of the Culinary Institute of America, is a twenty-year industry veteran. His early career highlights include working with Dean Fearing at the award-winning Mansion on Turtle Creek in Dallas as well as a stint as executive chef of Napa Valley's lauded Auberge du Soleil. Sutton is now executive chef of Napa Rose, the premier restaurant in Disney's Grand Californian Hotel, where he specializes in seasonal menus featuring California wine-country cuisine.

HOW TO TAME A WILD BLENDER

★ ★ ★ ★ ★ ★ ★ ★ ★ ★ ★ ★

Making cold items (like smoothies and vinaigrettes) in a blender is easy, but working with hot liquids is a whole other game. Hot liquids will leap out of a blender, no matter how tight the lid, and I have seen many beautifully colored hot liquids propelled to every corner of the kitchen—including a beautiful chimayo chile red sauce that I was making for my wife when we first began dating. The stuff flew out of the blender minutes before she arrived, forcing me to do that tornado cleanup we all do just before company arrives. (The first glass of wine really tasted good that night!) I didn't know it then, but the trick to keeping the hot liquid in the blender is the *rev method*. To do it correctly, all you need is a piece of plastic wrap to cover the bender. There will be no flying mess, and it is easy to add ingredients. Here's how to do it.

STEP ONE: Place your hot liquid in the blender, but do not exceed two-thirds capacity. Cover the top of the blender container with a kitchen towel or plastic wrap.

STEP TWO: Rev the blender, using the pulse function. Place one finger on the on/off switch and one on the slow or pulse switch. Use short, quick blasts of power to start the liquid moving. In other words, the machine will sound like a motorcycle being started: *Rum, RRumm, RRRRRUUMMMMMMMM*. The idea is to get the liquid going around in small quick bursts; each blast of the pulse button should cause the liquid to move. The first should move the liquid only one full turn—hold your finger down for just a fraction of a second. Quickly now, the second burst should grab the carry-over speed of the first pulse and increase the speed of the liquid—hold the pulse button for a full 2 seconds. The third pulse should be longer than the first two to get the liquid traveling around the blender easily—a full 10 seconds.

STEP THREE: Turn the blender to low (or constant). Now that the liquid is traveling around at a constant speed, the speed can be increased without causing the liquid to jump. This method will add air and make your soups and sauces lighter and more refined. Fresh herbs can be added at the end, lending color and flavor. To add the herbs, just lift a corner of the plastic wrap and drop them into the blender.

MORE CHEF'S SECRETS . . .

FM: You work for Disney; who's your favorite Disney character?
AS: Sebastian the hermit crab in the *Little Mermaid*; he can sing and he is always running from that crazy chef.

FM: Favorite ingredient?
AS: Love and purity. It sounds corny, but what that means to me is that the farmer cares for the ingredient, making it the very best, and then entrusts me to care for it when I cook.

FM: Prized cooking item?
AS: I love so much about being a chef that it is hard to choose just one prized item. I rebuilt my kitchen in our home and added a six-burner industrial stove—that and a great sound system have made cooking at home so much more fun. But the item that touches me the deepest is a killer solid copper pot signed by my team at Auberge du Soleil.

Hoppin' John Martin TAYLOR

★ ★ ★ ★ ★ ★ ★

PROFILE

John Martin Taylor, a.k.a "Hoppin' John," a South Carolina "sandlapper" who grew up casting shrimp nets off Hilton Head Island, is America's acknowledged Lowcountry cooking expert and the author of four books, including *Hoppin' John's Lowcountry Cooking*, the prototype for any serious regional American cookbook. In 1986, he founded Hoppin' John's, one of the country's few comprehensive culinary bookstores, in his hometown of Charleston. Converted to an online business, hoppinjohns.com is a culinary website and mail-order store dispensing regional recipes and ingredients for traditional Southern dishes to people all over the world.

HOW TO SEASON A CAST IRON SKILLET

★ ★ ★ ★ ★ ★ ★ ★ ★ ★ ★ ★

A properly seasoned cast iron skillet is strong and durable, with a nonstick cooking surface that conducts heat well, has a gorgeous shiny black patina, and will never rust. Forget the manufacturer's instructions about using vegetable oil. The only tried and true way to season a cast iron skillet is with lard (rendered fresh pig fat). It's really simple. If you go to a flea market, you might be able to find a pan that's already been well seasoned; it will be black and shiny and smooth inside. But for a new pan, bring it home and wash it once—the last time you'll ever wash it.

STEP ONE: Melt pork fat into the pan. Ask your butcher to grind enough fresh pork fat to fill the pan. Pour about 1/8 inch of water into the pan; then fill the pan with the fat. Put the pan in a 225°F oven or on top of the stove over a very, very low heat. Melt the fat slowly; it can take an hour or more.

STEP TWO: Remove the fat from the pan. When the solid matter (called cracklings) turns brown and sinks to the bottom of the pan, strain the fat through several layers of cheesecloth (or through a fine-mesh strainer) into a clean plastic container with a tight-fitting lid. After the lard has completely cooled, cover and store in the refrigerator. You now have home-rendered lard for pie crust and biscuits, as well as a seasoned skillet!

STEP THREE: Maintain the seasoned skillet. Wipe out the skillet, but never wash it again. After each use, rub the inside of the skillet with bacon grease and wipe out the excess. The salt in the bacon grease helps to preserve the skillet and keep things from sticking to the surface. If you must wash it, use cold water and a natural bristle brush.

MORE CHEF'S SECRETS . . .

FM: What makes Lowcountry food so distinctive?
HJMT: The food owes its flavor to the ethnic mix of the early settlers, but the biggest influence came from the enslaved West Africans, who introduced rice dishes, a spicy palate, and the stewpot cooking that would come to define the cuisine of the entire South.

FM: Bacon fat, butter, or olive oil?
HJMT: All fats, all the time! They're all traditional and they're all good; fats are the best carriers of flavor. The choice of which fat depends on the recipe. I can often date a traditional recipe (eighteenth to twentieth century) to within fifty years by the fat called for.

FM: Solve an old argument—gumbo . . . rice or no rice?
HJMT: What argument? Gumbo, from the West African word for okra, always includes the vegetable that gives it its name and is always served—as are most other local dishes—over rice.

HOPPIN' JOHN'S CORNBREAD

1^1/2 to 2 teaspoons strained bacon grease
1 large egg
2 cups buttermilk, at room temperature
1^3/4 cups cornmeal (preferably whole-grain, stone-ground)
1 scant teaspoon coarse salt
1 scant teaspoon baking powder
1 scant teaspoon baking soda
Butter to taste

Add enough bacon grease to coat the bottom of a 9- or 10-inch, well-seasoned, never-been-washed cast iron skillet. Place the skillet in a cold oven; heat the oven to 450°F.

Mix the egg into the buttermilk and transfer to a medium bowl. Add the cornmeal and mix well.

When the oven has reached 450°F, the bacon grease should be just about to the smoking point. Quickly stir the salt, baking powder, and baking soda into the batter, and pour the batter (all at once) into the hot pan. Bake for 15 to 20 minutes, or until the top just begins to brown.

Quickly invert the skillet to turn the bread out onto a platter and serve hot, with lots of butter.

Makes 8 to 10 slices, and serves 6

HOW TO REESTABLISH A NONSTICK SURFACE ON STAINLESS STEEL AND ALUMINUM PANS

★ ★ ★ ★ ★ ★ ★ ★ ★ ★ ★ ★

Stainless steel and aluminum pans are ideal for sautéing, especially when you're making pan sauces. Once you've learned to start with a screaming hot pan and a high-flash-point oil, you'll forgo those peeling nonstick-coated pans. However, at some point in time, even stainless steel and aluminum sauté pans become "sticky." The porous nature of the metal attracts contaminants and the pan needs to be cleaned. Here is how to reestablish a nonstick surface.

STEP ONE: Heat your sauté pan on high heat until very hot.

STEP TWO: Pour a generous amount of iodized salt into the pan.

STEP THREE: Swirl the salt around in the pan. The salt will clean out the pores in the metal and discolor from the impurities.

STEP FOUR: Discard the salt and wipe the pan with a clean, dry towel. You now have a clean, nonstick surface again.

Deborah KNIGHT

★ ★ ★ ★ ★ ★ ★ ★

PROFILE

Deborah Knight learned to cook on visits to her grandparents' bakeries in New Bedford, Massachusetts. Although she initially earned a degree in religion and anthropology from the University of Colorado, Knight later combined her childhood passion with her multicultural studies by enrolling at the California Culinary Academy in San Francisco. Following graduation, she did several restaurant stints in Boulder and Tucson, including working with her mentor Cary Neff at Miraval Health and Wellness Spa in the foothills of Arizona's Santa Catalina Mountains.

Returning to her hometown neighborhood of Pinnacle Peaks in Scottsdale, Arizona, Knight opened the globally inspired Mosaic, located on the edge of the Sonoran desert, where she rode horses as a child. She was named one of the 10 Best New Chefs in America by *Food & Wine* for her efforts.

MORE CHEF'S SECRETS . . .

FM: What's for breakfast?

DK: Well, as I am one who has never enjoyed getting up in the morning, and who much prefers going to bed in the early rising hours, I have never been much for breakfast. My normal routine is a cup of toasted brown rice and green tea. If I prove to be a bit more peckish, then I eat a bowl of miso with tofu and scallion or a nonfat yogurt.

FM: Best neighborhood joint, at any time?

DK: When I lived in Boulder I frequented on an equal basis three—Naryan's for Nepalese, Juanita's for Mexican, and Sushi Tora for Japanese. I have never had just one place—my preference has always been for diversity. Now that I own a restaurant, I have no time to eat out, so my current hangout is Mosaic.

FM: Favorite cookbook?

DK: My favorite is my first, given to me when I was six or seven by my parents when they returned from a long trip. It is *Meals of Many Lands*, a basic children's book of recipes from around the world. I think I made every recipe in it after I got it.

HOW TO KEEP COPPER POTS LOOKING LIKE YOU WORK IN A MODEL KITCHEN

★ ★ ★ ★ ★ ★ ★ ★ ★ ★ ★ ★

This great way of making a polish by utilizing food products came to me through a chef friend who said it cut down on cleaning-material costs and yet was an efficient way of maintaining a great kitchen look.

STEP ONE: Make the cleaning mixture. Mix 1 cup egg whites, 1 cup sea salt, 1/2 cup lemon juice, and 2 cups all-purpose flour to form a loose paste (adding more flour if needed). The paste will keep indefinitely in a sealed container in the refrigerator.

STEP TWO: Apply the cleaning mixture to copper or brass pans with a light abrasive plastic sponge and polish until any tarnish dissipates.

Andrew SABA

★ ★ ★ ★ ★ ★ ★ ★ ★ ★ ★

PROFILE

British ex-pat Andrew Saba has spent the last twenty-five years working in the Washington, D.C., area. He was opening executive sous chef at Marcel's, nominated for the Capital Restaurant and Hospitality Award as New Restaurant of the Year; he was also sous chef at the Watergate Hotel under the tutelage of the late Jean-Louis Palladin. Prior to his appointment as executive chef of the Jefferson Restaurant at Loews Jefferson Hotel, Saba oversaw the kitchen at the city's Tabard Inn, where he developed an eclectic American brasserie-style menu based on seasonal organic produce.

STEP THREE: Rinse with cool water and buff to a shine with a clean cloth.

MORE CHEF'S SECRETS . . .

FM: Ingredient you can't live without?
AS: Shallots.

FM: Best food city other than your own?
AS: London and Philadelphia.

FM: Most prized kitchen possession?
AS: Pair of twenty-year-old fish tweezers.

HOW TO CLEAN
A WOK

★ ★ ★ ★ ★ ★ ★ ★ ★ ★ ★ ★

Simpson
WONG

We didn't have an oven when I was growing up. Instead, my mother taught me to cook in a wok, and it is still an essential piece of kitchen equipment for me. The shape of the wok aids in the distribution and concentration of heat, and I even make my sauces in it. But the residue of cooking oils as well as the many sauces used in Asian cooking can build up, reducing the wok's efficiency. I want to keep the cooking surface clean, but I don't like to use strong soaps or chemicals. I rely on a more natural cleaning element—heat. Here's the trick I use to clean my wok.

STEP ONE: Heat the wok over a high flame. When a thick layer of cooking residue builds up, I place the wok (on its ring) over a high flame until it is extremely hot. Depending on the intensity of heat, the wok might change color, turning almost red in the center. It might also smoke a little and smell slightly like metal.

STEP TWO: Chip away the residue. When the cooking residue begins to form a crust (it will actually get crisp), the wok is ready to clean. Turn off the heat. Holding the handle of the wok with a sturdy potholder to stabilize the pan, chip away at the cooking crust using a flat metal putty knife (the thin, sharp tongue will work better than a cooking spatula), letting the debris fall into the center of the wok.

PROFILE

Simpson Wong learned his way around the kitchen by helping his mother prepare employee meals at his father's small timber company in Malaysia. A former banker and United Nations liaison, Wong has lived and traveled extensively throughout Asia and Europe and holds a decidedly global perspective on food. Skilled at bringing balance to his cuisine (no matter how far-flung the flavors can seem), Wong delivers a diverse but straightforward New American menu at his three-star restaurant, Jefferson, in New York City. According to the *New York Times*: "The America he has in mind is a diverse, equal-opportunity culture that thrives on immigrant energies. It's the America we live in now."

STEP THREE: Cool the wok under running water. When you have removed as much of the residue as possible, rinse the wok under cool running water. Then use a stiff bamboo or natural bristle brush to flake away the remaining crust. Now you are ready to start cooking again!

MORE CHEF'S SECRETS . . .

FM: How do you develop your interesting flavor combinations?
SW: I look for the natural community in food, even though the flavor connections might not seem obvious to the untrained palate. But I don't like to force combinations if the components are too disparate.

FM: Do you have a kitchen superstition?
SW: For the most auspicious cooking conditions, I mind my cardinal directions. My wok and cooking station always face south or east but never north or west. The north is associated with the cold, rain, and wind, which can "put out fire" and prevent proper cooking. Also, a feng shui master once told me that my personal energy is not receptive to the west.

FM: What do you cook when you want to relax?
SW: In the restaurant business, it is a luxury to take your time, and to relax I like to make leisurely dishes like slow-braised pork ribs with red wine, balsamic vinegar, and whole chiles, served with hearty vegetables.

TABLE OF EQUIVALENCIES

★ ★

FOR VOLUME

U.S.	Metric
1/4 tsp	1.25 ml
1/2 tsp	2.5 ml
1 tsp	5 ml
1 tbsp (3 tsp)	15 ml
1 fl oz (2 tbsp)	30 ml
1/4 cup	60 ml
1/3 cup	80 ml
1/2 cup	120 ml
1 cup	240 ml
1 pint (2 cups)	480 ml
1 quart (2 pints)	960 ml
1 gallon (4 quarts)	3.84 liters

FOR WEIGHT

U.S.	Metric
1 oz	28 g
4 oz (1/4 lb)	113 g
8 oz (1/2 lb)	227 g
12 oz (3/4 lb)	340 g
16 oz (1 lb)	454 g
2.2 lb	1 kg

FOR LENGTH

Inches	Centimeters
1/4	0.65
1/2	1.25
1	2.50
2	5.00
3	7.50
4	10.0
5	12.5
6	15.0
7	17.5
8	20.5
9	23.0
10	25.5
12	30.5
15	38.0

OVEN TEMPERATURE

Degrees Fahrenheit	Degrees Centigrade	British Gas Marks
200	93	—
250	120	1/2
275	140	1
300	150	2
325	165	3
350	175	4
375	190	5
400	200	6
450	230	8
500	260	10

INDEX

★ ★

ACKNOWLEDGMENTS

★ ★ ★ ★ ★ ★ ★ ★ ★ ★ ★ ★ ★ ★ ★ ★ ★ ★ ★

Thanks to my agent, Laura Blake Peterson, and her assistant, Kelly Going; my constant editorial inspiration and grammar guru, Jay Woodruff; and Dave Borgenicht, Melissa Wagner, Bryn Ashburn, David Stadler, and Jill Surkin, along with the rest of Quirk Books. I would also like to express my gratitude to the many fine food people (and their publicists) from all over the country who told their secrets for this book, especially Charlie Palmer, who embodies my idea of the perfect culinary cocktail: gravitas with a twist.

ABOUT THE AUTHOR

★ ★ ★ ★ ★ ★ ★ ★ ★ ★ ★ ★ ★ ★ ★ ★ ★ ★ ★ ★

Francine Maroukian, named one of the best private caterers in Manhattan by *Town & Country*, is the author of *Town & Country's Elegant Entertaining* and *Esquire Eats*, as well as a frequent contributor to both magazines.